GW01454203

Acknowledgements

My first wish is to offer my sincere thanks to Carol Cole who has devoted so much of her time and expertise to the development of the majority of this series of books. I also wish to thank Kelly Leonie Walsh who has likewise shared her artistic expertise with both design and presentation of all of the books. I would also like to offer my sincere thanks to Linda Smith for the help that she has given me in completing the last two books in this series

My second wish is a hope that many readers will uncover the '*Turning Point*', and in a way begin to look for further understanding in the path of your choice and discover the true purpose of life.

978-0-9569333-4-8

www.bernardfillayson.com

Turning Point

Bernard Fillayson

Published by Fillayson Publishing

INDEX OF CONTRIBUTED STORIES

I would like to thank friends who have contributed their stories to this edition. I wish to make it clear to readers that they are all perfectly true personal experiences or knowledge and have been given to share with others.

Turning Point

This book is a guide book and, like any guide book, it is not the places you visit but rather the direction in which you have to travel.

Readers will note that there are a number of short stories in this book. These are contributed by people with whom I have shared my life. Each depicts a story of an experience by that author. Each story has significance for the reader. The author wishes to offer his personal thanks to each contributor and their waiving of the copyright to their contribution. Any further use of this copy would be an infringement of this copyright. It is our hope that the reader finds the theme behind each story of assistance in their own life and may also learn from their own experiences.

In the final few pages of this book, you will find details of other writings similar to the words you have been reading or are about to read. These are a few reminders but each presents a different aspect of the work. Like *The Path Is Your Choice*, this volume contains personal contributions on life experiences by contributors and some re-quotes by the author. However, it is most important to understand that there are many messages therein and, as your life proceeds, you should really be taking these to heart in the light of progress, new aspects, new interpretations, and a wider understanding may evolve. May you not only enjoy your reading but also the understanding.

Introduction

Hello and welcome! It is good to be together for a short while. Please allow me to explain that I am neither a professor nor a prophet; just an individual like yourself. However, many years of meditating have granted me the privilege of sharing some of the understanding which I have received.

Starting with *The Path Is Your Choice* in which there are many short stories about life – anyone's experience from which vital lessons may be learned. Other books in the series take us along that path and offer a broader aspect of life; one which can answer many doubts and queries; which will help everyone to lead a life of great contentment and inward happiness.

It is important to remember that this usually takes place over a period of time, although there are instances of individuals who have received an almost instant self-realisation.

All these books have a life-lasting value. They are not dust collectors on a shelf. Their messages are simple and it is your privilege to receive those messages within them.

Buy one and try one. Sit down on a comfortable chair where you can enjoy a peaceful moment. Any help you may receive will be waiting for you in peace and tranquillity. Thank you.

–○○○–

There is a very simple way of looking at life. It is this: It is either lies or truth. Think on this for a moment. Now consider there are certain characteristics: light and dark; hot and cold; rough and smooth; and so on. All are held together by a supposed mysterious force – life and death.

This brings us back to the original statement concerning truth. We may wish to see this simply expressed as materialistic and spiritual, or form and formless, which, in one way or another, are explained in the true religions being practical at this time.

There are many people who say that they do not believe. This is because they do not see beyond the curtain of desire nor do they listen to the voices of the natural order. It is necessary to know that we are referring to proper listening and seeing beyond the obvious – i.e. beyond looking and hearing.

We all know that, between *black and white*, there are many shades of *grey*. Likewise, in life, until we reach the truly spiritualistic experience, there are many shades of living. We need to overcome these by an understanding of the Truth and obeying its precepts. Until we do this, practising repentance, life will be like being a load of dirty washing: put through the experience until properly cleansed.

Consider these words and take the *path of your choice* to reach and to develop your spiritual essence.

–o()o–

"Proof!" said the man on television. "That book is over two thousand years old. It is full of myths and fairy tales. How about hidden truths? It is arrogant nonsense like this that is so misleading."

The truth is this: what was the truth then is still the truth now for it never changes. This applies to all renowned teachings. To quote an example:

Whosoever lives according to the doctrine is very near
Buddha c. 500BC

–o()o–

The initials R.I.P may be seen on many gravestones in a Christian cemetery. It is a rather strange epitaph meaning 'Rest in Peace'. One is inclined to ask: But why not during their lifetime on earth? It is perfectly possible given the correct attention to self-determination, fully conscious of Being, and less to attachment.

—o〇o—

If the beginning and the end are together then the Spirit has chosen to do this.

—o〇o—

Ask yourself: Does habit overpower the case for need? In this manner, one does not recognise the need.

—o〇o—

There are two wild cats that come on to the terrace at regular intervals – twin sisters. They are lovely, and they receive breakfast in the morning and a late afternoon meal of cat biscuits. It is noticeable that each of them enjoys the privilege of nuzzling in on their sister's food plate. One wonders if this is also a human trait, and the reason why there is so much sadness in the world – for each cat had an adequate sufficiency of food in its own bowl.

Misunderstandings, if left to fester, can lead to devastating consequences. It is better to seek reconciliation than revenge.

—o〇o—

It matters not what anyone may say, however high the personage may rank, but, for a fact, your life is a gift, just as the body is a gift to enable you to learn and become a better spiritual entity. Treasure both. Do not squander them or rudely cast them aside in the face of the Beloved.

—o〇o—

How large is the space that you occupy?

–o()o–

How humanity doth deceive itself:

The sky's the limit – well now we know this is just not so. Space is a vast not yet fully understood phenomenon.

Time is of the essence – which of course is total nonsense. Time is, as it were, attached to manifestation and not beyond.

Money is the root of all evil – so where, for example, does jealousy come in?

The sun sets and the sun rises – this is laughable. The sun shines all the time.

Acceptance is the beginning of awakening to what is. Think on this: you take a walk in the countryside and decide to pause. You sit down on a nearby rock. All is very peaceful. Then a bird begins to sing. You listen carefully. That occupies the moment which is present. Then the bird stops singing and that peace which was is still there. It has not changed. Within that peace is the manifestation of what is (the birdsong). What occurs next is what is; there is no future in it. Should you be able to understand this, you also grasp the fact that one can only act effectively by being in the present moment.

–o()o–

When asked about smoking, the man paused for a short while and then said, "I really enjoy it" without realising that smoking (nicotine) was actually taking him over as he had lost control of his habit. This is not only about smoking. We need to be in control of all our habits or they will control us.

—o()o—

Look for a solution in your own soul
Daniel Barenboim, orchestra conductor

—o()o—

That which is written down may often conceal the truth. Often it is the case that, if you want to find a precious metal, (i.e. like the hidden truth), one has to create a mine to find it. It is hidden under the surface of the earth. Likewise the message of Truth.

—o()o—

Misunderstanding may easily be explained – that it is like the running waters running wild. What starts as quite a minor problem develops into something much larger and far more damaging if left to its own devices rather than preventing it from developing incorrectly in the first place. The cardinal rule, if there is such a possibility, is to sort it out at once, with sensible dialogue. Remember that, without this form of dialogue, mistranslation from one individual to another can have devastating results.

—o()o—

This I learned from the shadow of a tree that to and fro did sway against a wall. Our shadow-selves, our influence may fall where we ourselves can never be.

Anna E Hamilton

This is a beautiful statement for at least two reasons: Firstly, by watching a happening carefully, we may learn something so very important it could affect the rest of our lives. Secondly, do we really realise the effect of our 'shadow' activity connecting with the lives of others?

There are thoughts and then there are after-thoughts about now and then. Then happened long ago so now is all that is left.

—o〇o—

A thing of beauty is a joy for ever.

John Keats (1795 – 1821)

An inspirational phrase which is as true NOW as it ever will be. This applies to this world for within its ONENESS is diversity, but the joy within it is enormous if one can only find it. If we could only travel that far in our small and short orbit, we would find the beauty which it is.

It should be remembered that a THING is NO-THING until it is created, and the love in creating makes it beautiful.

—o〇o—

Seek beauty in nature
Find beauty in nature
Close your eyes slowly
Find beauty within yourself

—o〇o—

Thieves broke into an English public park one night and stole a bronze statue by one of Britain's most famous sculptors of the age. It was sawn off its base and removed by lorry. It would be taken away and sold for its base metal price. Metal prices then were very high.

Consider for a moment the actions of these thieves, their destructive and demoralizing contribution to society, and thereby lies the question of what was becoming of that society. Consider how the pleasurable and aesthetic quality of life for many thousands over the age had been wantonly destroyed for such a paltry sum. Basically, there is more to life than money although that has its uses.

—o()o—

The key to any successful relationship involving marriage is to keep the vibrations in melodic form. One might say like two hands on the piano producing a harmonious sound or vibration. The more perfect the harmony becomes, so the more beautiful the sound.

—o()o—

The moment of Truth was before you
The moment of Truth is in front of you
Look – listen – and obey

—o()o—

A very great number of people are unconscious of their worth and thereby unfulfilled in life. It is important for everyone to find out what talent is buried within their unconscious state and thereby participate in the fullness of their lives. Were this to be so then there would be far fewer discontented persons amongst us.

—o()o—

She heard that her friend had murdered his girlfriend because she had been unfaithful to him. Her feelings expressed were those of amazement in that, for the first time in her life, she could visualise the underlying anguish of what happened and remembered the biblical saying: *Father, forgive them for they know not what they are doing*. The actual cause of this sad affair lies much further back in life than in the immediate present. One may also wish to remember the underlying background of the original fault.

—o()o—

As one grows older and older, one really wants less and less in terms of material possessions. In the end, the inevitable is the Eternal.

Sit down and be comfortable. Here are a few questions you may wish to answer. You may want to write down your answers.

Are you the body that you think you are?

If you believe you are the body then ask how did I make myself or, if it was made for me, by whom was it made?

What keeps this body alive?

Surely the answers lie somewhere else, outside the body itself in the sense that the energy source is not of the body structure itself?

So, what is the powerhouse and where does it exist?

—o0o—

Why are we spending so much money on space research when we need to cultivate more space on earth for those who live in poverty? Surely this concludes that humanity has got its priorities all wrong?

—o0o—

Everything is perceived where no thing is. Love, joy and happiness abide in this no thing and are therefore in every thing. Take the covers off.

—o0o—

The message is quite simple and applies at all times and in all states:

Abide in Me as the outgoing tide recedes, and you will understand that I am what I am.

—o0o—

Where Truth is, there are no alternatives.

—o0o—

He who bakes the bread
Can also eat his own loaf

—o()o—

That which lies beneath the topsoil can often be discovered by the will to dig a little deeper.

—o()o—

The wave of his content is on the surface of the underlying cause and is fanned by the wind of change.

—o()o—

Young boys when by the sea often play the game of pebble bouncing. This game is not only interesting in itself but, looking a little deeper, it should also give the player or those who are watching an indication of the meaning of life itself.

Firstly:

One chooses to play the game. Then one has to find pebbles with a flat surface.

One decides which path to take so it is necessary to decide that which is important.

Next:

The correct position for throwing. The pebble is thrown so that the flat surface bounces along the surface of the water.

One stands by one's choice. One sticks to that decision. The energy one releases carries the idea forward in various stages until it expires.

The pebble bounces across the water and eventually sinks as the energy you applied is exhausted. But each contact leaves a ripple which expands beyond the initial point of contact.

Each idea develops its own potential and expands to include other subjects connected to the original.

Eventually the pebble, energy expended, sinks into the water.
Eventually the idea is overtaken by new ideas.

The game shows that. Given the right conditions and energy application, work may proceed. As it does so, the effort affects those around it.

–o()o–

Do not jump to conclusions. Consider the facts first.
It is not what you do that matters; it is who you truly are that counts.

–o()o–

In Japan, an undersea earthquake may often cause giant waves to hit the coastline and cause devastation and loss of life. In one such case where over 15,000 humans lost their lives and a whole landscape fifteen miles deep was devastated, it was noted that all the animals and birds had fled to higher ground long before the destructive waters arrived. In Spain, it has been noticed that many garden birds depart their areas before a heatwave descends upon the area. Is it not interesting to note these examples of Nature's awareness? One asks oneself: *Then why did so many people die in that tsunami?*

Hold on; we might consider the great bird migrations to their nesting grounds. Then there is the long trek of the herds in Africa to feeding grounds further north. If that is not enough, how do salmon know where to go across the Atlantic or ocean whales travel thousands of miles to their breeding waters?

All this understanding gives us a basis for thought.

–o()o–

Approaching the crossroads and traffic junction ahead, the area was clear of traffic. So, whilst enjoying a little natter, the driver drove on. About halfway across, she realised she had passed a red light. Fortunately, amidst some hooting of car horns, she drove the car safely to the other side without further incident. But, **what if** someone had started to cross the road? **What if** the cars starting to lead the opposing queue of traffic had accelerated more quickly?

Yes, there are *what ifs*. But what about *All you need is before you*? Will the lesson to stop talking so much when driving – pay attention to the job in hand – be learned? Will the lesson be remembered the next time, or does it need an accident to wake the driver up? Give full attention to the job in hand.

—o()o—

He telephoned the office of the retirement home and requested a wake-up call for 7 am. But, surely, this is what most of us need all the time? We are living in a daydream.

—o()o—

If one allows the blind to lead the blind, there is 'no knowing' where they will go. Similarly, if there is 'no knowing', one gets nowhere of any significance.

—o()o—

The aeroplane crashed into the ocean with the loss of 289 lives of passengers and crew. The authorities were able to salvage some of the wreckage. After examination, the investigators concluded that neither the pilot nor the two co-pilots flying the aircraft were able to interpret the warning signs of problems being relayed to them through the instrument panels in the cockpit. It is similar to situations arising in everyday life. If you are 'asleep' and do not read the information given, you will not achieve a successful, happy and contented life. Be aware! All you need is in front of you.

–o()o–

Should you give due credence to the primary requirements in life then your life will be in tune with the Universal Will of the Creation and become much happier.

–o()o–

The one person you cheat is yourself for you make believe yourself to be what you are not.

–o()o–

He who kills another in the name of his religion simply dies within his own self.

–o()o–

Now, this requires your undivided attention:

The flowers and trees which flourish in tropical climates differ from those that grow in temperate zones. Be aware that the clothes worn by those who live in tropical climates differ from those who live in temperate zones. That is obvious, you say. Well, note that the flowers and trees do not fight each other so why should we argue over our different religions so long as they offer the same natural Truth only in a different way.

–o()o–

If your ego is so paramount that you are unconscious of the cruelty and futility of your actions then you are lost, even to your own self. Only by seeking first and foremost that state of spiritual consciousness can you receive forgiveness and the understanding of the knowledge.

–o()o–

Be mindful of intelligence; it has a great deal to tell.

–o()o–

Hidden by the clouds of the ever thinking mind is the enlightenment of the Spirit in consciousness and love.

–o()o–

We are all human and have a lot to share and a lot to learn … whoever you are, whatever you do.

–o()o–

In one sense is solid and yet in another is fluidity.

–o()o–

Do you live in a state-room
Or is your room in a state?

–o()o–

Can you see through the 'Mists of Time' for they are part of the illusion?

–o()o–

For those who are down-hearted
Try to be up-beat

–o()o–

You may read something but do you understand the meaning behind it? Perhaps it is not unlike cooking a meal. You may do the cooking but it is eating the meal that is the result which is the criteria.

–o()o–

The poet wrote: Beauty is in the eye of the beholder. As beauty is always there, what does this tell you about the eye?

Let's go ego-bashing

The ego is one great problem. Remember what was said many years ago: I am the greatest. Piffle! Believe it or not, everyone is the same only different, for we judge by the primary state and not the secondary and ephemeral state. In the primary state or True Being, we are all the same, but in truth this Being may be covered over in others whereas, in self-deception or secondary state, we believe we are better than or worse off than others.

–o0o–

Trust once lost is gone forever
But truth is never far away.

–o0o–

We can all accept that a body is born with nothing and dies with nothing. Can we accept that a body is the same wherever it is born? All bodies are just a form referred to as a body. Parentage and birthplace may well have an effect on size, shape, colour, and similar factors may well have an effect on the form, but a body is still just that.

It is the formless life-giving creative force which is so important. It is this which formulates, combined with the environment which dictates the actions and attitudes of that form. Thus, from any point of view, it is the cultivation of the formless invisible part of nature's creation which dictates the action of form. All this is replicated in the use of automobiles and aeroplanes, the bodies of which do not function without the suitable fuels.

–o0o–

Only the eyes can tell
Beauty of bloom

–o0o–

Action 'off the cuff' has little reason
Life is but a glimpse of love.

–o()o–

It is useful to remember that anything which has been discovered was always there. What else can we find?

–o()o–

Family

Mum, Dad and the family, a young son and daughter, were all sitting at a table outside the café waiting to be served. The young son spotted an insect crawling across the table and, with one finger, carefully nudged the creature. Whereupon Dad, in a calm and tender voice, said, "Now you be careful of that, Danny. Remember it has family too."

Anon

As the hour repeats itself, so does history.

–o()o–

Enjoy life by living rightly, but do not possess it, for it is given to you and can certainly be taken away.

–o()o–

To be still, be upright.

I had to do it.
I wanted to do it.
It really made me feel good.
It needed to be done.
And it helped them.
What will you be giving?

History is in the present day, no matter where
you are or who you are.

–o()o–

As it is necessary to know when and where to change trains,
so it is necessary for all of us to know when it is necessary
to change direction.

–o()o–

How many of us studied history whilst learning at school?
It really does not matter particularly whether these studies
had a national or international background. So often what
the ordinary individual was given were the dates of births
and deaths of people referred to as important; events and
their conclusions in favour of one side or the other. But
the real point of learning is so often glossed over by the
majority of us. It is this: History, like everything else is
cyclic by its very nature, and a study of its nature will give
us a clue as to what may arise today.

–o()o–

All you need to know is before you. There is always a
choice. Taking that choice is what you make of yourself.
Listen for the answer in Truth.

Bring two ends together and there is no end.

It is said: *Still waters run deep*. How about a still mind?

–o()o–

Do you really know what other folk really do for you?

–o()o–

The passing of a body is a matter of fact.

–o()o–

Love is eternal; possession is ephemeral.

–o()o–

It is an interesting thought, is it not, that children have to be taught about danger to themselves before any possible dangerous situations occur.

–o()o–

The Helping Hand

It was a warm and sunny day. So some friends and I decided to go for a swim in the sea.

Unlike nowadays when most young people have an easy opportunity to learn swimming, in my young days finding a location where one could be taught was not quite so easy. So, I have not found swimming to be a sport in which I enjoy the experience, and any aptitude has therefore suffered the result of neglect.

There is now no excuse for anyone's inability to swim. Parents have a certain responsibility to ensure that members of their family learn, not by being thrown in at the deep end but through close and careful encouragement.

Anyway, I digress. Back to the sunny day. We all set off and in due course were playing and frolicking in the light surf. I was trying to swim to the best of my ability parallel to the shoreline when, all of a sudden, I discovered I was at least one hundred to two hundred yards away from the group. Try as I might, I could not make headway back towards them.

Then I saw on the shore a large board advising swimmers not to swim in the area in which I found myself. I was caught in the current and did not have the talent to overcome it or swim out of it. My colleagues were a distance away, too absorbed in their games to notice my absence, let alone hear any cries for assistance. The beach was becoming further away by the minute, and it was then that I realised that I was incapable of helping myself any longer. The only thing to do was to pray. This I did, saying, "If it be Thy will, please help." I had hardly finished when a wave came and lifted me up, and carried me to where I could touch the sandy bottom. I struggled ashore rather exhausted. After finding my breath, I walked along the beach back to my friends and joined in with their games.

Whenever I recall this incident, I can still feel the hand in that wave lifting and carrying me to shore, and firmly believe that my prayer was answered.

Bernard Fillayson

First published privately, subsequently in
The Path Is Your Choice 2008

How many folks become 'caught up' in the struggle of everyday life and find it so difficult to uncover a way to calmer waters?

—o()o—

A Lady Walked By

Still was the evening, I stood all alone
On the flagstone steps in front of our home.
Pastel the colours that painted the sky
And there in the lane a lady walked by.

On a gable end rooftop neighbourly nigh
A young thrush was singing without feeling shy.
Each sound as it travelled through infinite space
Cast a bright light on this ordinary place.

Never before had I heard such a song
Each note in its scale so rounded and strong.
It's hard to express in any known word
The beauty conveyed by such a small bird.

I listened intently in hearing this call
And suddenly realised that space contains all.
Those melodious notes which this bird had sung
Were a sharing of love and life all in one.

No longer, no longer was I all alone
I stood in a presence containing my own.
Freedom from worry and a wondering why
And there in the lane that lady walked by.

July 1996 First published in a private edition
Verse and Verity by the author

The Dream

Let not the horrors of our time dictate your mood
Full fleeting are the many troubles of this world
Crass fear doth cause a dread of such events
True faith and love shall bring a calm content.

Just look upon this life as an apparent dream
Reality appears when true awakening comes
Still consciousness doth hold all things in place
Misjudged ideals lead to a useless chase.

What e'er befalls, consider it a message sent

To enlighten or maybe cause one to repent
True knowledge will depend upon a conscious state
A measure of control on what some say is fate.

May/June 1996 First published in a private edition
Verse and Verity by the author

—o()o—

Love in – mind out

—o()o—

Why is it called 'never never land'?
Because folks never really try to go there.

—o()o—

Nothing matters. It is what one does with 'nothing matters' that matters most.

—o()o—

As has been indicated in another volume: 'The only embodiment which knows the whole Truth is Truth itself.'

—o()o—

Sex is not love; sex is the Creative Principle applying its energy to the reproductive power of matter. Used with sensitivity, it can produce sublime feelings in human nature. It can also be selfish and demeaning. The pure energies of love reach far beyond this.

—o()o—

Who do you think you are?
The ephemeral form of the ego?
The spiritual searching for the Creative Principle?

—o()o—

The nature of all beauty is the Creator.

—o0o—

The awareness is in the pure consciousness of every human being. So have you discovered it?

—o0o—

So, listen to the voice in the breeze,
It has a story to tell.
Just do as the Great Power pleases
And power will be given as well.

—o0o—

Now, be honest with yourself. Have you really considered how fortunate you are? To be gifted with life? Or do you just accept it, forgetting that you are that being in the natural garden of delights.

—o0o—

There is only ONE WAY.
All the rest are side turnings.

—o0o—

Many years ago, my wife needed to have a very serious abdominal operation. Her life had become one of great misery and pain. The day after the operation, the specialist came to visit her at her bedside and asked how she was feeling. On hearing that she already felt a different woman, he said, "Well, don't worry. We have taken away the carrycot and left you the playpen."

This joke reverberated around the dinner tables for some while afterwards until, quite gradually, it dawned on us that this saying had a far deeper meaning: stop carrying around all your troubles and prejudices, petty hates and the like; get up and play life to the full; full of joy and happiness and love.

It really is not strange to say that that was exactly what my wife achieved for not only herself but also for all those around her.

—o()o—

Two helpful rules towards a contented and happy life are to hold to a balance and keep everything simple.

Let us look at one example. (Many readers will know of this already):

The seas and oceans cover 72 per cent of the earth's surface. The water, also in depth, together with the lakes, rivers, etc keep the physical in general balance in caring for the population, providing they behave themselves. This is a question of balance.

Then we have the sun warming the waters lifting moisture from the waters and forming clouds which, when heavy with water drops, fall as rain back to the ocean through rivers and the seas to the source of their origin.

The energy from the sun creates this cycle.

—o()o—

Human beings in bodily form are born, live a life and then die, and the form-factor returns to its source. But, and this is important, what drives the bodily form? Surely there is a formless energy or electron magnetic force which drives the body during its life cycle. This is the spiritual essence of a human being; this is the beauty and love of the Creator. Always there; always waiting for YOU to seek its benevolence, but covered over by the 'my and our' ideas. We need to go beyond this curtain.

—o0o—

Fools rush in where angels fear to tread.

—o0o—

Complaints

In Forum, a residential home in Spain, there are many foreigners living permanently as guests in this country, and we already take it for granted that there is always some sunshine warming our worn-out bones. Surely all of us have some kind of pension which allows us to pay for our daily costs.

In this country of Spain, we don't need to escape from war as thousands of people have to do in Africa. Here, we are never woken up by tanks as they are in Iraq or the Yemen, no Arab Spring; yet there are times we don't feel happy not even content. It may be due to a crisis within the family or because of the pains in our bodies caused by the passing of the years, rheumatism in our shoulder, a sudden attack of lumbago or because of the chronic degeneration of hips or knees. Many times even less important things cause anger, e.g. when a dog keeps barking, the noise of the rubbish van at night. Even the singing of the birds in front of their windows early in the mornings disturb some residents' sleep… some of them would prefer to see the trees cut down. And a few wouldn't mind getting rid of the crickets in the trees whose noise at night annoy them. Every day, we can complain if we want to find something that doesn't please us in this life like a street lamp which isn't lit in the evenings, or a lift that doesn't function when you need it, or the faded white colour of some pedestrian crossings, and of course nobody likes prices going up the way they do.

Last week, I sat on a bench at the beach of Albir looking at the blue sea. Everything was calm, relaxed, quiet; the weather, the landscape, sea and heaven formed a perfect peace. Tourists sauntered along the sea front. A middle-aged gentleman pushed the wheelchair of a young lady, a beautiful young girl. He sat next to me on the bench. They were British and spending a fortnight of their holidays in Spain. We talked for a long time together. His wife had lost both her legs at an early age through a traffic accident and was now only twenty years old. But the face of the young woman beamed with happiness; her shining eyes reflected the joy of life. One could feel it, see it in the gestures of her movements when she spoke, and hear it through her words. Her inside beauty impressed me. "Many people who can live here permanently seem to have forgotten how privileged they are and how good life is towards them," she said and continued, "but I do not envy them. We are not as rich as they are in order to be able to live here, but each day is a gift for us and we enjoy every day wherever we are. At this moment, we are here and love spending our yearly holidays here in Spain. Life is good for us. Others aren't as fortunate as we are. I am happy and grateful for my destiny. I thank God every day for my life." I admired her.

Anon 2013

It is a fact of life that if one always looks at the positive effect, life will respond, and even the apparent negative will offer a lesson to learn and improve the moment.

—o()o—

Live and let live. That which IS.
Every aspect just IS.
Here is an obvious statement: Wherever you go, you are
there. But are you? Let things be and work from there.

–o〇o–

The Failure Of His Life

One day, at the Friday market, I met a man I had known for twenty years. In those days, he owned a leather shop where he sold Spanish shoes and materials from his own factory. His type of business did not allow enough free time for him to spend much time at a flea market.

"What are you doing here?" I asked, surprised to see him. '"You're not busy with your business in Benidorm?"

"We haven't got it anymore, not for a long time," he confessed with a sad look.
"What happened to you? Was it the fierce competition of the Chinese?"

He smiled. "No, that was the reason many of my neighbours' businesses closed, but that is not what happened to me. I simply made a mistake – the failure of my life," he replied thoughtfully.

I did not ask more. If he wanted to tell me, he would do so happily showing trust in me. Failure to do so, I thought next minute, he could consider it was none of my business and that I was just being curious.

He looked at me for a while, fighting his own emotions.

"Let's have a drink and I will tell you." He had finally decided to speak and certainly spent a long time telling me almost everything about his life. "When the business was going well, I thought it wasn't enough and still wanted more: a larger mansion, a farm in the mountains, and even a private yacht fifteen metres long. All this cost a pretty penny. But I was convinced that I could pay for everything; also, all the expenses that I would have in the future … But times changed suddenly. First we had to let the staff go, and my family and I worked in it ourselves until we needed to sell the store. The situation was getting worse, so we were forced to sell our mansion losing money. The ship we had to sell for less than half of what it had cost. As if that were not enough, my wife left me and took the kids. Today on the farm I live alone, and I'm thinking about the possibility of selling fruit from the farm at the market here, but I see so many people doing the same, now I do not think it's worth it … and that's why you see me here today," he muttered, embarrassed.

I tried to comfort him, giving him a long list of human errors to show that similar things had happened to a million people. I knew it was not going to help. How many millions of euros were lost on the stock market or in construction in Spain? He knew it himself. "Think of the poor in other countries who lost everything by earthquakes or tsunamis. Think about the people who are hungry and thirsty, and the millions of human beings who live in abject poverty under dictatorial regimes," I said.

But he had already thought about it himself. All this could not comfort him. "Everything you say is part of people's fate, but mine was just my own fault. It was my greed that produced this. Greed was the failure of my life."

"We all make decisions in our life! And commit errors!" I told him.

"No, you do not convince me. I understand everything you say." He shook his head.

"I see you've dissected everything that's happened, but think one thing: how many people over a drink caused an accident and killed someone or even themselves? That was also the failure of their life, but they are dead and you aren't. You live. Look around you, look how much life there is in this small market, how it developed during the crisis. For you, there is hope. Make plans; you can still achieve your dreams. You're not sick. You still have much to live for. Now you know your weakness and the worst of your personality and that you can fight to change the part of your character that has caused 'the failure of your life'. You still have many possibilities to start and feel alive again. Many others are left with nothing, not even life."

He bowed his head and said no more…

Gisela Corty

The Little Boy

My partner Martin and I had recently moved to a lovely little house in the picturesque village of Albir, Costa Blanca. The house is an older type, with a patio leading off the lounge and into a little garden. My lifelong friend Sue was staying with us for the week and, as it was getting slightly dark, I lit all the candles on the table and the scented oil lanterns. Being August, there was no breeze but high humidity so we were spending every evening on the patio. The atmosphere was jolly and relaxed, and we were talking as we ate our meal. As I turned to speak to Sue, I got such a shock and let out a shriek as I saw a boy of about five years old standing beside me stretching his arm across the table, and his head was turned towards Sue. The next second, he was gone. I wasn't frightened in the least, but shocked. Sue thought that I had broken a tooth as I was eating; my face must have looked a picture but I can only hope I see that little boy again. His hair was so thick and shiny in a kind of long bob.

Lorraine Swailes

Many sceptics would attribute this experience to hallucination. For me, it is an indication that there is another world out there with different wavelengths of life.

☞ Forgiveness

About fifteen years ago, I had a life-changing, spiritual experience. At the time, I was attending a sexual assault class regularly, for things in my past I don't need to mention. One night, lying in bed, I came to the realisation that I would have to forgive my grandfather for what he had done to me (and my sister) for years so that I could move on with my life. A battle began raging inside my head, and I was suddenly feeling panicky and distraught. I knew I was in such a conflict with myself that I started having a panic attack. A HUGE one! I was beside myself with fear and confusion to the point of almost fainting. I was feeling trapped and terrified when, suddenly, to the left of me in the darkness of my bedroom, Jesus came through my wall and stood at the foot of my bed! I was mesmerised. I have never been a religious person, yet I was dumbfounded by his presence; the incredible love I felt coming from him; and the light surrounding him and my room was beyond anything I had EVER experienced! He smiled at me; he held out his hand and gently turned his body to look behind him, at a globe, the Earth, spinning in my bedroom! He didn't say a word to me, yet I heard what he had to say to me … He looked at the Earth spinning, about the size of a medicine ball, turned back to look at me, and said telepathically, "I have forgiven everyone, from the beginning of time, for EVERYTHING they have EVER done." As I continued to stare at him with amazement and feeling the hugest love I have ever felt, he smiled at me again, the globe disappeared, and he walked out of my room through the wall at the bottom of my bed. I realised, after a period of time had passed for me to digest what had just happened, that HE had forgiven my grandfather, and so could I! It took me a while, but I did manage to forgive him. This experience changed my life. I'm still not religious, but very, very spiritual. I asked for a spiritual path after that night, and I received one. Not without its bumps and holes, its ups and downs, but I know without a doubt, Jesus existed, exists to this day, and loves us all like we could never imagine.

J

In the Christian tradition, one of the commandments says: Thou shalt not kill. (This presumably refers to other human beings.) In most countries referred to as 'civilised', sanctions are taken against anyone who kills his neighbour. Even if a man starts a fight with someone else, he is censored in one form or another. How come, therefore, one should fight at all? One form of belief against another? If it is wrong to kill, why do religious leaders mislead their adherents? Surely we still have a great deal to learn. Energy expended in this direction is better directed in other directions of goodwill.

—o()o—

What is the point in becoming possessive of objects? Enjoy what you are given, but you cannot 'take it with you'. Surely the stories of the pharaohs and the well-stocked pyramids of three thousand years ago tell us that, so can we take anything? Manifest objects: No! Those formless spiritual deeds which are held in memory are carried forward. So, remember this.

—o()o—

Inanimate objects: If you break a cup, another has to be made. Neither can it reproduce itself. Someone else has to make a new one.
Animate objects: Can reproduce themselves but there has to be a male and a female aspect. However, how does the action work? Surely, there has to be a higher intelligence. What is that?

—o()o—

This story has been printed elsewhere but it is a valuable insight into the inner being, and there are no qualms about repeating it here. It was told to me by my wife Jilly about thirty years after the event.

As a very young lady under twenty-five years of age, she had been working in a London office for two years. This office lay midway between two London train termini – Victoria and London Bridge. In those two years, she had always taken the train to Victoria but, as she stood on the platform on this particular day, a thought came into her head and persisted – *take the other train today*. So she watched the Victoria train arrive and resisted the idea of getting into a carriage. As the train left, there was the feeling of *What am I doing*? and, as the next train was for London Bridge, she caught that one and hoped she would reach the office on time. She did.

A short while later, after she had arrived at the office, she received an anxious telephone call from her mother enquiring if she was in the office and whether she was all right. News on the radio had just announced that the train to Victoria had been involved in a terrible accident in which many of the passengers had been killed and a large number seriously hurt. It was, in fact, one of the most serious accidents that particular railway company had ever suffered.

One must question who issued the warning to this young lady, and how fortunate it was that she had the strength to perceive it.

—o0o—

How many men still remember hunting the beach for a suitably sized flat stone and then, finding one, tried to bounce it across the water. Even to drop an ordinary stone into the water of a lake, pond or sea provides a lesson for us all. One stone sends ripples across the water. The flat stone, if properly thrown, can bounce for five or six times sending ripples round each bounce. Consider therefore an analogy of this story to the words you may say to others on the advice you may take at any one time. How far do the ripples of that action go? Everything one says or everything one does in life has a ripple effect from the source of that action. Mark my words! used to be a well-known expression. Would you get good marks?

—o()o—

Freedom of speech does require distillation of speech.

—o()o—

In the world of form, when truth starts to be required, spirituality begins. There is a loss of egocentricity, and an expression of true love begins to emerge. In the longer term, however, love develops, and togetherness in the shape form-less. Togetherness merges into Being and all is Love.

—o()o—

Our practice changed. Thinking became still, and an awareness took over with thinking becoming the servant of the experience.

—o()o—

The 'here' and 'now' is where you are.

—o()o—

Now is the hour, the time to say goodbye
To the thoughts of what I want
To those of what I need, and do away with clutter.

—o()o—

Surely many of us know a little about how the dinosaurs existed and died out. In one sense, it is more interesting to consider how they came to be there in the first place.

—o()o—

Looking back through history, it is interesting to consider what humanity has learned and forgotten in the years of our development. Considering the wonders of nature and even of ourselves, we are not very good pupils.

—o()o—

If you do not do something NOW, you will stay where you are today.

—o()o—

There is a well-known saying: *Never put off until tomorrow that which you can do today*. Each week we read the freebee newspaper and, as we walked into the supermarket, we noticed a large pile of the latest edition. As I bent over to take two, my helper said, "We'll collect them on the way out." Of course we forgot, and this meant that we had to make a special and unnecessary journey later that day to obtain the particular new issue. Quite simple. Do what one has to do NOW.

—o()o—

Is it not so that someone who has been upstaged will say to the other person, "Who do you think you are?" In fact, it is a question they should be asking themselves.

—o()o—

We used to meet each other at a weekly study group and became quite friendly. He worked in one of London's great auction houses and specialised in porcelain. I had a personal interest in a number of small emerging businesses. His knowledge of his subject was good, and I was interested in acquiring some pieces as an attractive investment. One day, we agreed to take a short break in Bruges and see if we could find anything of interest. I paid for the trip and, on the last day, seeing something in a shop window, he disappeared into the premises and returned with the purchase. It was sold in the next auction and paid for all the expenses of our visit. This impressed me, and I offered to finance a small objet d'art business if he agreed to participate. He agreed. So I purchased a new car and gave capital for the purpose. Meanwhile, I noted that he had appeared on the BBC's *Antiques Roadshow* and was duly impressed. However, his success was his ruin. He became involved with the wrong company and indulged in riotous living; smashed up the car and was divorced by his lovely wife. I picked up the pieces and never saw or heard from him again – what a tragic waste of talent.

—o0o—

Can you be honest with yourself and say, "I have enjoyed the work I do and have done all my life."?
If not, ask these questions: "If not, why not, and what did I do about it?"
There is a very old saying that is: *Work is a labour of love.*

—o0o—

WHERE YOU ARE IS JUST THAT.
Where you want to be is where you are.
Do not add anything to this presence.

—o0o—

Unless you fully know the circumstances
How can you satisfactorily reason on the consequences?

—o0o—

My Friend 'V'

My friend 'V' and I are both Christians and we each have leadership roles in our respective churches. A few months ago, 'V', who is no longer a young lady, had a terrible accident. It was only when my wife and I were at the hospital bedside that the full horror became apparent. 'V' had been working in her split-level garden and was severely injured when she fell some three metres onto a paved area. Her left leg was broken – which was bad enough – but her right foot had been almost completely severed. I saw a photograph of the injury and was amazed that, even in what must have been a state of shock, 'V' managed to use her mobile phone to call for her own ambulance!

By the time we got to the hospital a day or two after the event, the situation had worsened. 'V' had been told that a severe infection had set in and there was a possibility that the foot would have to be amputated. At the very least, 'V' would have to face months of skin grafts, confinement to bed and a long haul through physiotherapy before any weight could be placed on either leg. As she lives alone, she would need live-in support at her own expense and faced the prospect of her busy life being put on indefinite hold.

Most of us would have been utterly depressed at the thought of such a future, and I, for one, would have been thinking 'Why me, Lord?' or 'What have I done to deserve this?' Imagine my surprise then when 'V' said, "I have been so blessed by this experience." When asked how she could possibly say this, she replied, "Well, firstly, the Lord gave me the strength to hold on as I fell, which saved me from landing on my head; and secondly, I have been able to do so much for Him from this hospital bed." The private ward was always full of visitors of all ages and nationalities who mostly came from 'V''s large and lively church. 'V' explained that, although she was well known within the church, there were some visitors who were less well known to her. Some of these people had problems of their own, and 'V' said that, whenever she wanted to pray with them privately, it was as if the Lord had prevented medical staff and other well-wishers from entering the room!

To further illustrate the power of prayer, 'V' is making

steady progress. A second opinion, change of hospital and an inexhaustible rota of helpers has enabled 'V' to improve her physical condition. Never far from her laptop, 'V' has stayed in touch with family and friends, and the ability to maintain many of her church activities has kept her mentally alert. Her spiritual and emotional needs are anchored in her faith and are expressed through the love and prayers she shares with fellow believers. Her indomitable spirit and infinite patience has been exemplary.

Now, whenever I feel the need to look for positives in a seemingly totally negative situation, I shall just think of my friend 'V'.

Peter Adams, Javea, Spain

This Christian viewpoint can be appreciated by many with other faiths.

—o0o—

Consider for a moment that the energy in your life is the same force which moves everyone. It follows, therefore, that if you hurt any other person in any way at all, you are hurting yourself.

—o0o—

There is nothing but love.
And that nothing just is ... all.

—o0o—

There is a saying: *Loves makes the world go round.* The Creator is love and, in the creation, the world goes round.

Beyond and behind that is a beyond in which the real Truth lies. It has no boundaries.

—o〇o—

Now the secret of my own happiness, my own good fortune, is within my own hands. I must not miss that opportunity.

Buddha

What really matters?

Let us pause for a moment and give brief consideration to the world in which we live and ourselves within it. Perhaps the first consideration might be to accept that this world, whatever we may think, was not made by us, neither do we own it. It has been given to us – humanity – to live and work in. Then again, we are born to live in it and pass away. Apparently, we are born with nothing and dissolve taking nothing away – that is, of a materialistic nature – so it could be said that the body is a gift to us. Like the Breath (we do not provide breath), this is just another gift given so that the body can function.

So this leaves the question: Who is the we/us? – for whilst it appears to come with the body, it does not appear to be a part of it, and yet it is most certainly with it. Is it not the functioning force? Often referred to as spiritual?

Here we are as part of humanity as humans or human beings. Functionally, these two are different: one acts for its own ends and the other acts in the knowledge that to be or not to be is the question; that there is more to life than fighting for material gain – what I want; what I desire; what I fear. Whereas in Being, there is belief leading to faith, trust and an ever evolving improvement in life's development which comes with Being.

So we can ask ourselves: *What is the point of it all?*

To start with, we might find the answer in the Christian teaching of the Lord's Prayer: *May Thy Kingdom come on earth as it is in heaven.*

This does not mean that this is the purpose set for humanity; nor the one of personal gain, rape, pillage and self-aggrandisement through war and destruction. Other well-known and respected religions teach similar ethics.

This prayer in the Christian tradition does answer another point: ... for Thine is the Kingdom ... – not only in heaven, and this covers the first part of our consideration – to leave the temptations behind and work for the good and benefit of all.

–o()o–

Let us look at a few more words from the Christian tradition. There is the Holy Trinity: God the Father, His son, Jesus Christ and the Holy Spirit – Three in One. So we have the Creator, human experience and the spiritual energy force.

In the Lord's Prayer, it is said: May Thy Kingdom come on earth as it is in Heaven.

Now, who says "My body" or "This body is mine"? No, no. Did you make it? Did you buy it? Is it on loan? – more like it. So if it is a loan, do I drive it? Do I create the breathing? No. So, is this the Spiritual Force at work?

Do we have an outer force which drives us and an inner spiritual force which guides us? One driving force going one way, and another force going the other way. So when we die, the force in the body departs and the materialistic body then returns to it source, the Spiritual Force, the earth.

So have you or anyone else created a heaven on earth?

–o()o–

Be still for the presence of the Creator. The joy in life is resting in the arms of the Creator, practising the talent you have been given.

—o()o—

When little boys found out about little girls, they became more interested in bigger girls. When people find out about the beauty of nature, they become more interested in the natural understanding of life.

—o()o—

A moment of kindness – a true story

There is today a lady living in Spain on the Costa Blanca whom I shall call 'J'. She used to be a Roman Catholic nun – a lifestyle that she followed for thirty-five years; travelling around the world, involved in many Christian projects.

One day, she decided that she actually did not really know God and the teachings of Jesus Christ. She left the convent order, moved to Spain and joined an international Baptist church.

The church has a decent-sized congregation and has various outreach events. One of these is a walking group where the church members are encouraged to bring along non-Christian friends.

I am a regular member and 'J' used to walk with us. One day, in late autumn several years ago, we went inland to the mountains near the former leper colony of Fontilles. As we walked into a village at about 3pm, we passed three elderly Spanish ladies working in an allotment. They only spoke the regional language – Valenciano.

After coffee, we retraced our route from the village, past the three ladies. One of the ladies was sitting on a roadside stone, shivering. 'J', who spoke no Spanish, went over to speak with her in English. I stood back and waited for 'J' to rejoin our group. 'J' spoke quietly to the lady whilst placing her gloved hand on the lady's shoulder. Then, as I watched, she took off her gloves and gave them to the Spanish lady. Shortly after, she said goodbye to the three ladies, turned and walked over to rejoin me.

As we set off, I said to 'J', "That was a very kind gift that you gave to the Spanish lady."

She replied, "Thank you, they were my mother's gloves – they were the last items of my mother that I possessed. But the Spanish lady needed them more than me!"

Marcus J Russell, Broadstairs, UK

Bees work before the sunlight fades away.

–o()o–

Can you believe in yourself? Can you believe that everyone is born with a talent; this talent to slot into life's intricate structure. Pause for a moment and think on this.

The young man was frustrated. He felt he could paint but did not have the wherewithal to buy the necessary equipment. Egged on by a friend, he got a job as a refuse collector, saved up some money, exposed his talent to the world and became a renowned artist.

Then there was another fellow whose work was to drive a coach carrying people on holiday tours. Through hard work and initiative, he became the proud owner and CEO of a national coach company.

Mohamed the great prophet was an illiterate nomad, and Jesus Christ was the son of a carpenter. What inspiration and power in the way of love and understanding did they provide?

On the understanding that your hidden talent can be of benefit and of help to others, build on it. One does not necessarily think of oneself. For instance, there are others such as Martin Luther who opposed the authoritarian regime of the Catholic Church and changed the face of religion. Mahatma Gandhi, the Indian, protested over many years for the rights he believed the Indians deserved. Then one has the unselfish and unknown individual who touches the hearts of those in poverty anywhere in the world.

It is not always a question of working for personal wealth, but for the betterment of human society as a complete social entity.

–o0o–

A little unselfish kindness travels a very long way. Usually out of sight to the provider.

–o0o–

Some people can be dead even though
they are actually alive.

–o0o–

Be wise in your listening, or misunderstanding may occur. Listen to that which the other person says and not to the interfering mind.

–o0o–

As the gentleman had problems walking, he requested his

companion drop him off at the door of the hospital and then park the car. So, while the companion waited, he decided to go inside and, as he did so, the electronic doors obligingly opened. Inside he waited and, at that time, a lady exited through the same doors and, stopping in the porch, fumbled in her large bag for a mobile phone. Leaving the bag in the crack of her arm, she dialled the call and started to talk, thus leaving her right arm free to gesticulate up and down emphasising her every point. Up went her arm and the electronic door opened. Down came her arm and the door closed. Up went her arm again and the door repeated its action. The woman, obviously oblivious of the door, repeated her gesture several more times with the door opening and shutting on each occasion.

Is this not a lesson for us all? Appearing amazing at the time but, in seriousness, do we really understand what effect our actions have on others or events?

—o()o—

Whether our ego accepts the situation or otherwise, we need to begin with an acceptance of what IS.

—o()o—

Find comfort in looking
Find comfort in listening

—o()o—

Dogma is the tragedy of self-opinionated thought.

—o()o—

You know what you have to do, but do you do it?
What is true?

—o()o—

He was a millionaire, but still very poor.

His pockets were full, but his true mind was empty.

—o○o—

Pleasure is of form and ephemeral
Happiness is of spirit and everlasting

—o○o—

Master! Please be my guide and my strength. I realise you are here, there and everywhere. Please open the gate to Thy Presence. Please guide me to help others as Thou hast helped me.

—o○o—

Are you like the apple which is hard and tasteless or that which is soft and uninteresting?

—o○o—

Some beginnings last longer than others
Some endings last longer than others
But we do not own any thing at all
All, including life, is on loan

—o○o—

Now is the hour
Now is the time to live
The past has no departure date
The future no arrival date
Stand fast and be ready
Stand up and be ready
To meet the moment NOW
NOW is the beginning
NOW is at the end
NOW is always there

—o○o—

As a child, one is taught to do one thing at a time. Have you lost this very valuable instruction? Give attention to what you are doing at that moment.

Become tender-hearted and level-headed. Allow the love of human kindness to know without thinking.

Give and it will be given unto you.

A smile goes a very long way.

Your mind is a statement of your experiences. Still the mind and let your thoughts subside in peace.

Stillness can arise. Become fully conscious of the origin of all splendour.

–oOo–

Allow life to flow; then start to grow.

Do you give yourself space, or use up that which you have?

Are you with it? What IS?

The ego (eg personality – *I did it all by myself!*) acts as a closed door to pure consciousness in space. It is not 'I am aware'. It is being aware of awareness. It is no-thing; it just IS.

Creativity arises within you; the wise consciousness within oneself.

The wise man prayed and said, "Everything I have is Yours." Right action comes through You and not of You. Umpteen years ago, there was a popular song entitled *Never say never again, again*. Like the general approach to life, this is negative. Try and adopt a positive attitude in your thoughts and action.

–oOo–

As a cub reporter, the local newspaper sent him to review the travelling circus which had recently come to town.

A marquee had been erected, but the seating had yet to be installed. The ringmaster gave him a seat and asked him to watch the rehearsals, then asked to be excused. The reporter soon became absorbed by the performances he was watching. As he was taking notes, he suddenly realised that outside the ring where the seating would normally be, there was a silence. Whilst he was sitting quite still, he realised that the performances he was watching were also in this silence. As this awareness arose, it was interrupted by the arrival of the ringmaster who came to enquire if he needed any more help. On his return to the office, he was congratulated on his perception of the assignment he had been sent to cover.

–o()o–

You gesticulate, you speak, walk and maybe nod your head – all body actions. Maybe you recall your heartbeat or even, on occasions, your breathing. But what about the stomach digesting, the kidneys or liver at work? How often do you feel these working away? You may even think and recollect that the mind helps you to fulfil life's task, but how about believing that behind all this is a spiritual power which has an everlasting and firm foundation unlike all the other matters mentioned which pass away in the course of time.

–o()o–

We should not trivialise the power of thought. It is through thought that our actions are formulated. So let us keep to one thing at a time, and not become muddled. So many problems arise out of muddled thinking – believing one thing was meant when another thing was said.

As human beings, we are far from perfect, and this results

in so many of the problems we are called upon to face up to – to learn to become better, to improve. The first thing we have to accept is the natural world – a world of form with all its wonders and beauty. Next we must accept that its place in the Creation. Together with those varieties in conditions and circumstances which this implies. So there are differences in the natural resources, the environment and specific condition.

Now it is known that a young body and individual at about the age of two to three begins to recognise its surroundings, the actions of others and so on. It is not difficult to assume therefore that certain characteristics within that body person will begin to be formulated. Remember, it is still human and it is the conditions that are going to play a major part in the development.

The simplicity of these thoughts indicate to us that, although our bodies arrive in the same birthing manner, differences in culture will arise.

Pausing there, let us turn to a wider field of development, for we begin to understand that which we observe and in which we exert a much wider, powerful and wondrous phenomena. We begin to realise that fragility of our being, and turn towards this superior power.

Religions have been born. Let us take a look at some of them. It is not within the scope of this story to deal with every civilisation that we know to our knowledge even existed.

–o0o–

We need to understand that we have to accept everything as it is at any given moment and move on from there. The wonderful evolutionary process works in all its wondrous ways. We have to learn to play in a positive way within it; otherwise there are distressing consequences.

—o0o—

Knowing

It was a busy morning, about 8:30, when an elderly gentleman in his 80s arrived at the hospital to have stitches removed from his thumb. He said he was in a hurry as he had an appointment at 9:00 am. The nurse took his vital signs and had him take a seat, knowing it would be over an hour before someone would be able to see him. I saw him looking at his watch and decided, since I was not busy with another patient, I would evaluate his wound. On exam, it was well healed, so I talked to one of the doctors, got the needed supplies to remove his sutures and redress his wound. While taking care of his wound, I asked him if he had another doctor's appointment this morning, as he was in such a hurry. The gentleman told me no, that he needed to go to the nursing home to eat breakfast with his wife. I inquired as to her health. He told me that she had been there for a while and that she was a victim of Alzheimer's Disease. As we talked, I asked if she would be upset if he was a bit late. He replied that she no longer knew who he was, that she had not recognised him in five years now. I was surprised, and asked him, 'And you still go every morning, even though she doesn't know who you are?' He smiled as he patted my hand and said, 'She doesn't know me, but I still know who she is.'

Anon

Stay right where you are for that is the place to be. Just be that One-self.
Just be as you are. Rest in the peace which surrounds you. Just be that One-self.

Who looks? Who listens? Be quiet. I'm looking! I'm listening!
To the voice that may be heard
To that which is the ever-giving word
In that moment one may surprise One-self in a study of the listening and the looking too.
I am looking, I am listening to the gifts that Nature gives and helps as it lovingly provides.

—o()o—

You are what you think you are, or are you one who knows who you truly are?

—o()o—

Everyone wants to be ahead. Why not stay where you are? Everyone wants something. Why not accept what is? What is it you deserve? Who is the YOU?

—o()o—

Beauty is a natural gift and loving thoughts a part of it. Sharing it is also the same. Have you really ever asked yourself: What is progress? Is it growing up? Is it satisfying a want? Is it being aware all the time? Is it being peaceful?

—o()o—

The harmony in beauty is for everyone to see.

—o()o—

When the time is right, are you aware of the need and the consequences? There is one army cliché used when referring to a fellow soldier who has been brave in battle: 'He covered himself with glory.' Most of us cover ourselves with a cloud of 'unknowing'. We pay more attention to material factors and this blinds us to the True Reality of getting to know the One True Self.

—o()o—

In a television interview some time ago, a woman stated quite emphatically that she did not believe in God. Of course, she is not alone, but one has to ask what she does believe in – maybe nothing at all. One can, of course, have a strong belief in oneself in relation to the everyday activities in life. Looked at critically, this is an attitude of self-indulgence and is really insignificant in the order of existence. Further, of course, it has no lasting capacity. It is agreed that those with such facile ideas maybe do a lot to help others, or do they? Surely one needs to understand the True Nature of this Creation. Marvel at its variety and productivity. Then ask how did it commence and how does it function? Two simple questions can help to provide a basis for questioning the non-belief theory and to ask a physical question: What sustains or even starts your breathing, and why does your heart go on beating? In very basic terms, these are essentials over which you have no control – only if artificially applied – but then, what is Life? Those who experience nothing have missed the very essence of Life itself.

—o()o—

Scientists advise us that the universe was probably several million years in the making. We do know from history that we can trace the human existence on the planet to a few thousand years ago. This brings us down to our present era. Meanwhile, science and physics, with the development in photography, its equipment and the development of the human race, show that there are hundreds and thousands of different species on this beautiful planet. You could pose the question as to how all this wondrousness came about, and how it is maintained over these many, many epochs.

As humans, we pride ourselves on our abilities. There are those who achieve 'greatness' in one form or another. Many seek to find some of the wonders of the Creation so let us ask ourselves this question: What matter is there already? We did not produce it, did we? Our existence as a human being is what? Eighty to ninety years? Rather miniscule when one compares this with what has gone before. The universe runs itself. We have terrible egotistical ideas of our importance as a world traveller. What if our place is as a silent reformer rather than a bragging, impertinent, egotistical human? We become lost in the insubstantial, the fleeting and non-essential, whilst the blessing of that inner life, of beauty passes us by. Peace deludes us although certain elements can remain.

–o〇o–

There were two young tortoiseshell kittens that, with their mother, came to our terrace in the retirement home searching for food. Their presence was a strong reminder of how we all rely on sustenance for our bodily requirements. Some of us visit the food stores whilst others like to eat in cafés, snack bars and restaurants. The availability of sustenance for our bodies from any of these locations should also be a reminder that there are others in this world who are not so fortunate, and sharing to help those not so fortunate folk is a better part of human nature. Every moving physical object needs some form of energy force to enable it to function. If we just acknowledge ourselves as bodies then the food which we require is sustenance enough. If, however, we acknowledge that there is another energy which motivates our daily lives, a spiritual energy, then we need to remind ourselves that it is necessary to seek this and to learn how best to do so.

–o〇o–

What is religion? Is it something which people anywhere in the world have either been taught to believe and accept, or is it something which has the basis of what one might say is an advanced state of the human experience?

Would we not accept that primitive man felt that there was something beyond his lowly existence? One might say the power of good or evil. They performed the necessary ceremonies accepting both their needs for protection from wild spirits and help towards a secure life.

As life progressed, peoples began to accept the presence of various gods for different purposes or the presence of an Absolute and Supreme Creator. These ideas were expressed in the religions we accept in modern times. Exponents of this ideology have resulted in the elevation of certain individuals who have undergone transformation to arrive at a level and explain in their experiences the basis of their teachings. There are many with creative ideas, some more well known than others. Nevertheless, effectively, although their method of teaching may differ, they all acknowledge the presence of a Supreme Power with the Universal Creation.

To be practical for a moment, and yet being brief, peoples in this world live in different climates; they speak different languages; wear different clothes; and eat different foods. Being brought up in these different circumstances therefore, they may well view the same phenom in a different light to others, though they may well be seeing the same light.

Accepting therefore, because of human nature, there may be false prophets, we are inclining towards the acceptance that there is just One Creator and, in our different ways, we are the seekers of the Truth. What follows is neither strange nor funny. It is what happens in life.

As just one possible example, let us travel from London to Istanbul in Turkey. There are innumerable choices:

Travel by air
Travel by coach
Travel by car
Travel by ship
Even walking or cycling

The choice one makes is dependent on many circumstances: e.g. air or seasickness; available capital; the wish to see parts of Europe, and so on. All the above follows normal everyday considerations.

Can you accept that there are different procedures that all lead to reaching the same destination? Does this answer your question of diverse religions leading to the same destination?

There are different ways to reach the same destination, and one should be tolerant and understanding of the needs of others. If one is properly geared up to a certain level of simplicity then the foregoing script can start to be understood. From previous readings, you will appreciate that there are always some individuals who will pronounce 'judgement' proclaiming their contrary ideas, their 'knowledge' to be correct. The Truth is simplicity itself, and that is what we seek.

You will always find a counter-argument. This is the basis of human existence. To look at it in the most obvious terms is probably the best way to commence our consideration. There is man and woman; day and night; hot and cold, and so on and so on. But argument as clearly mentioned in prophet Omar Khayyam's book never achieves anything. So, in fact, there is only one true way – the way of Self-Realisation – the return to the Creative Source.

Ensuring one is pursuing the correct way forwards

is the foremost priority for mankind. It is not Self-Aggrandiscment. As we have said, it is Self-Realisation. Realisation of the Truth in Creation. Not in the way of the world but in the Path of Truth and Love.

—o()o—

Judgement

Do you judge another person before you judge yourself? What is the force of the egotistical personality trait? What right has anyone to pronounce judgement on others before perfecting themselves?

—o()o—

Do you ever wonder why you were born into the world? Was it to acquire riches and fame? Or to get what the little 'I' wants? Or possibly to be of assistance to the will of the Creator in making this world a 'heaven on earth'? Or is it to satisfy our own sense of possession and greed? How many of us respond to that still, small voice which is calling us to pray?

—o()o—

Everyone is given what they need at that particular time. This is all they can manage. They do not need anything more.

—o()o—

The past is a lesson not to be indulged in. The future will never arrive. For NOW is the only moment that exists. The consciousness changes what is to come.

—o()o—

There is so much to do
And so short a time
In which to do it.

—o0o—

Are you placed on this earth
To do your own will
Or that of the Creator?

—o0o—

The awareness is ever present beyond the casuality of past and future thought. It is a complete presence in the NOW.

—o0o—

Many words record the surface waves of their expression but seek the underlying meaning.

—o0o—

The beauty of love is in the giving and sharing. Both share the beauty. It is like a lifelong beautiful flower which never dies.

—o0o—

The following copy has been reproduced from a monthly news sheet issued to the occupants of a retirement home. Whether you feel these techniques are difficult or strange is of little consequence – what is of importance to us all is to realise that this is only one of the factors of agreement between teaching. Further, if you look in the right direction, one can find the guidance that is needed.

Food for the Spirit

The Bible states that laughter is a source of health. It reads: 'A merry heart is like a good medicine, but a depressed spirit dries up the bones.'

Some Hindu books even speak of meditation by laughter, and the fact that laughter is a meditation technique in itself, while it is an effective way to learn more about yourself and also will help you become more aware of the world around you.

In India, Bhagwn Rajneesh (Osho), in his centre at Poona, promotes meditation of the mystic rose consisting of nine days with three hours of laughter each day, while some Buddhist schools teach techniques for smiling whilst walking about and says that it is as beneficial as meditation or even more so. There is also a Hindu belief that an hour of laughter has more beneficial effects on the body than four hours of yoga.

The most persecuted peoples are the ones who have a highly developed sense of humour, and that's the Jewish people. The Chassidim were religious teachers who understood that religion should not be so sad, and they had some humour, songs and dances injected into religious rites and into life in general.

The Chinese philosophy Tao also promoted laughter. An old Chinese advice says that to be healthy you have to laugh thirty times a day. Experts say about three times a day is sufficient if it is for more than one minute on each occasion. The psychiatrist William Fry, who has studied the effects of laughter for more than twenty-five years, says that three minutes of intense laughter is as beneficial to health as about ten minutes of rowing vigorously. He also says that one minute of laughter is equal to forty-five minutes of daily relaxation.

It costs nothing to smile at someone, and that smile will be worth a lot to the recipient.

Maria Maltseva, Spain

My wife once told me a story of an incident which took place in the family home when she was a young girl. This story is so simple and, to me, so compelling, I feel it is worthwhile sharing it with others.

The family would finish enjoying breakfast together and, between that time and the time to depart for school, the father might say, "Have you fed the birdies yet?" Yes, quite simple and so gentle, but what a lesson … You have finished your meal but remember there are others who may need to eat as well. In fact, it helped a young girl always to remember the needs of others.

More than fifty years after that event, we were still feeding the birdies, and, I hope, remembering the moral of the story.

Many, many years later, when we were married, we purchased a villa in Spain. The front garden was quite narrow, say four metres, and in the middle we had planted a small acacia bed with a bird bath in the centre of this bed. Birds would line up on the small iron railing atop the front wall and take it in turns to fly down to the bath, have a quick 'shower' and then fly off, allowing the next participant to arrive.

Many of us will know of some of the great pleasures that Mother Nature shares with us. What more is there to life?

—o()o—

Lao Tze has a saying:

We must be able to be at peace in order to be active in love.

Now just think for a moment. These words are not very profound. In fact, their message is very obvious, but how many uphold the truth in, say, governing today. Is greed not an overpowering factor in the hands of those who wish to succeed?

—o〇o—

There are weeds in every garden. Unfortunately, not everyone is a good gardener.

—o〇o—

It is said that history repeats itself. Does this mean that humanity never learns? Of course, man may learn and forget but, without forgetting, man may learn. Sometimes, forgetting means forgiveness.

—o〇o—

If you have one another, what more do you want? Or what more do you need?

—o〇o—

Everyone wants more – greed. Everyone has a need – wanting can become greed. Need is all important because, by satisfying that need, one becomes a better person.

—o〇o—

For just over forty years, we enjoyed the friendship of Alan and his wife Mary. They had two sons: the elder became a top business executive and the younger enjoyed a more placid, happy family life.

Alan was a few years older than myself and was unfortunate in that his father died when he was still at school. When the time came for him to leave, his mother advised him to find a secure job 'for life' with a pension when he retired. So, he found work with a very well known insurance company. Three or four years on, World War Two commenced and he was called up to serve in the Royal Navy. He distinguished himself and was presented with his decoration at Buckingham Palace by King George VI.

After the war, the family lived in a small detached house in a beautiful corner of Kent. Alan enjoyed caring for a good-sized vegetable plot in the garden. Eventually, he received his pension and retired happily. After a few years, he passed away never having really distinguished himself in his business career. I was not able to attend his cremation but visited his wife soon afterwards when we discussed his life as described above.

"Hold on a moment," she said and left the room, returning with two magnificent cut-glass vases, proudly explaining that the workmanship was solely by her husband.

I could hardly believe this. I had never known of his talent. The vases were exquisite. Here was a talent completely unknown to me and only barely exploited.

In later years, I found myself wondering how many people actually find their true talent, or do we just job along in life, or become caught up in a frenzy of just existing. This begs the question if anyone can be happy, truly happy, if they never find the talent which is theirs.

—o0o—

Nurturing the next generation

Whilst out enjoying an afternoon stroll along the beach front, sun warming my back, embracing the ambience of an idyllic family day, I took note of a family in the seated park area enjoying the facilities: everyone enjoying a drink, and the children delving into their weekend ice cream treat, all interacting with each other in a normal, relaxing way.

After everyone had finished their refreshments, the children went over to the play area where the swings, climbing frame and slide were. I assumed the fun was to continue. Meanwhile, back at the table, the adults, Mum, Dad and Grandma, all reached for their mobile phones and sat for at least fifteen minutes, not a word spoken between them, and sadly the same scenario was unfolding in the play area with the children. None of them played: they mirrored their parents and reached for their phones and gaming devices, happily playing without any interaction. These children were aged between five and eleven years old.

Parents need to be aware of their behaviour and the impact it has on their children's development.

You cannot escape the consequences of your actions. What you do comes back to you.

Be not deceived; God is not mocked, for whatsoever a man soweth, that shall he also reap.

Galatians 6

Linda Smith, Perth, Scotland

Do not be misled by those teachers who choose to enhance their own ego rather than help the undernourished in Truth. Their words are a falsehood.

—o()o—

There can only ever be One Truth and this
applies to everything.

—o()o—

All the great prophets devoted their lives to others rather than enhancing a self-opinionated idea of themselves.

—o()o—

Right now you need to know who you truly are, but this self-realisation should never become covered over by thoughts of who we think we are.

—o()o—

Many years ago, after the start of the Industrial Revolution, steam engines, locomotives and ocean-going liners were powered by the application of fossil fuels. Following on came diesel oil, also an extraction from the earth. At all times, human beings were instrumental in controlling and directing the machines they had constructed. For a moment, ask yourselves where was the power which enabled human beings to do this? Consider for a moment: the body of any human is really not different – it feeds on natural resources to keep it alive and promotes its activities. So we need to ask ourselves: is all the required activity performed unconsciously or do we accept the conscious reality that a supreme spiritual power grants us, as human beings, the power to enjoy what is really a minute part of the universal entity? Surely, within our inner being, there is an untapped power so poorly acknowledged that we find ourselves lacking in complete love and understanding of the glories and beauties of this extraordinary universe.

What is the difference between life and death?
Transition

—o()o—

Surely, in the twenty-first century, mankind has gained enough experience to realise that there is one complete Truth in life and that this is compounded by love. Surely mankind has realised over the centuries that greed and self-gratification are not the way forward to a better world. Surely any right-minded adult must know that no tree is the same in its growth and that the same applies to the human race. Alternatively, weakness should not provoke cruelty; rather pity, help and understanding.

If people set out to go on a journey from one location to another, they may use different forms of transport and go by different ways. Should they suffer from a mental or physical disability, this will have a bearing on their choice of travel. We all have different abilities, and those of us who have been fortunate to have received greater learning should be willing to share this with the less fortunate. Cruelty in any form is a sign of brutal repression and corrupt practices.

—o()o—

Fine, we agree that some folks are a menace to society and should be deprived of their freedom.

—o()o—

Truth cannot be changed; it just IS.
Likewise the *present moment*.

—o()o—

It is better to enhance the eco system
than the ego system.

—o()o—

Whether our ego accepts the situation or not, we have to begin with an acceptance of what IS. If one moves into a new home and the house is dirty, the situation has to be accepted before anyone starts to clean.

—o()o—

We can share our bodies (form) but more important is the meddling of our souls (consciousness).

—o()o—

An empty jug has no contents. Likewise an empty mind. Be careful with that which fills the space.

—o()o—

Every wheel has a hub, and every spoke has a purpose. Maybe the rim is a long way from the centre. Maybe the rim is on the hard track. Where are you in this analogy?

—o()o—

Nature, of course, can advise you on so many things in life. One simple example is that of the seasons:

Spring – *the time of new life and rebirth*
Summer – *the fullness and fruitfulness of life*
Autumn – *the slow down of activities*
Winter – *passing over to rest and build-up of energy*

We need to remember that the tree does not die. All that which life inspired rests within. Likewise with self-conscious regenerations.

—o()o—

Religion is not about persecution or execution. It is about absolution and resolution/revelation.

—o○o—

Elsewhere in this book, we have considered the rainbow and its message. Now let us consider another aspect of the Creation. If you study everything in the room or place where you are sitting, you will envisage many forms and colours. Take all this away in your mind's eye and all that is left is original space. Space has no form; it just IS. And within that space, creation is formed. We now know from the development of civilisation about the radio waves, TV waves, etc. These have a multi-functional purpose but, for example, when two people fall in love, they are said to be with similar thoughts or on the same wavelength. Is it not so that, if a person falls in love, this is a formless abstraction displaying itself through form and, being on the same wavelength, they are mutually compatible? This then shows up in the shape of the forms between the two. This is perfectly recognisable, and so long as they continue to share the same form-less 'identity', they will always be in love. Otherwise, they become incompatible. Therefore, in the case of marriage, for example, the formlessness has to change together so that the form can survive in any given situation.

—o○o—

In temperate climates, we experience four main climates with adjacent locations having variants of these defined conditions. The year commences with Spring which is birth and renewal. Summer is the season of growth and rejuvenation. Then Autumn arrives, and the life expresses its time of expiration with leaves falling and changes in animal behaviour leading to Winter. Now, consider the position of human beings. They are born in the Spring; develop their lives in the Summer; begin retirement and slowing down in the Autumn. When Winter arrives, they pass away. However, consider for a moment that the sap in every tree rises to bring new life. Is our sap renewable?

You do not have to DO anything
Just LOOK
Just LISTEN
And you will know what you have to do NOW
The finer POINT about this is that you need to KNOW how to do it.

–o()o–

Whilst living in Spain, an Englishman arrived at the doctor's on time for his appointment but was kept waiting for over thirty minutes whilst others were being attended to. Eventually, his interpreter made a mild protest which received the reply: "We treat the Spanish first." In one way, this may be so, but we all have a need and are not really that different in our needs.

–o()o–

Frequently forgotten today is that honour and trust are so fragile that they have to be handled with great care. Not only are they fragile but they are also extremely valuable; an intangible value beyond price for the stability of life depends on them. *Yes, yes*, they say, *we know all about this*. They may know all about it, but do they honour it? Do you trust them so to do? When one comes to think about this, then it is really quite difficult to tolerate a lack of trust, and why one should have to consider such thoughts anyway.

–o()o–

Have you not found this to be true? If you hold on to or possess a gift, present or possession, after a certain time, it takes hold of you.

–o()o–

For those folk who consider that earth matter is all that there is, let them ask themselves: within what does this earth matter move?

Is part of your life spent exercising your ego? If so, you will find it harder to know yourself.

—o○o—

If you do not believe, you may never know in life – and yet, there is always a chance meeting or a mystical greeting in the awareness.

—o○o—

Every end has a new beginning.

—o○o—

Time – a popular misconception. It does not actually exist but has been invented by humans in order to regulate their lives in the manifest world. In the latter respect, of course, it works. This is a difficult concept to accept, but means now that everything happens in the present moment. That is gone and another present moment arrives. That is what IS.

—o○o—

Realisation

The true interest in life does not lie in discovery and knowledge but in realisation.

Teilhard de Chardin – Towards a New Mysticism
Ursula King *Seabury Press (New York)*

What is realisation? That which Teilhard de Chardin had to say may seem to be contradicting; in one sense, that is, in the meaning of the words. So let us look at these words from a particular point of view.

Starting with realisation: This is the understanding of one's True Self together with the mystical aspects of this world in which we have been given our lives.

On the question of discovery: Surely it is not difficult to conceive that any discovery by man is really an uncovering of that which is already there. As this uncovering takes place and proceeds then the wider aspects of the Will become more apparent.

Now let us examine knowledge: Knowledge is generally accepted to be those items of information which one gathers during the course of one's life, e.g. concerning science, history, mathematics, and so on. However, again there is a greater knowledge – universal knowledge. This is far, far greater than the generally accepted learning which is treated as knowledge. It is the unveiling of the miraculous, the unseen and the true world of the Spirit. To find this out, we need to seek the Truth, and this means finding a teacher or school of teaching.

–o()o–

Silence

Yet what was there when parable and paradox failed to produce the state of grace which was the dawn of enlightenment? There was always the world of nature that in its heart nourished the sympathy deep in all things for one another, which 'The Great Artifice' denied.

I was woken by the silence. The sound of the rain had gone and nothing had moved in to take its place. It was the sort of silence that used to be called 'absolute' and is seldom part of contemporary life. There was nothing frightening about it but something so positive that I thought of it as a trumpet call to the day.

Laurent Van de Post (1906-1994)
Yet Being Someone Other

Here Van de Post relates one of the problems facing so many people today.

Parable and paradox have lost their meanings and the 'sound' in the silence has almost been forgotten. In fact and deed, both need to be resurrected in order to lead to understanding, peace and greater love. One could possibly start by applying the biblical parables or teaching of the Sufi masters to experiences in modern life. There are lessons to be learnt from many ancient scriptures that provide answers to the present-day problems which face mankind.

The need for all of us to seek a measure of silence is a vital creative act. There are moments of silence between each one of the actions that we undertake in our daily lives. We should try and remember this. At dawn or eventide, there is time for reflection. However, it is the greater silence that we need to embrace, and, as the writer explains, we could start by an understanding of nature. Behind all manifestation, there is silence.

—o○o—

In stillness

Where stillness is, there rests a silent call to me
No tremor, stir, within befalls except from Thee

For in this vast all-knowing lies
A gently cradled world

It is as if the sun has no more writ
Upon our lives
But is an act upon a stage set in transcendental skies

For in this vast all-knowing lies
The mirage of our world

Knowing this all-seeing silent yet
Creative pulse
Such must be master and protector for
Each one of us

For in this vast all-knowing lies
The everlasting world

—o()o—

Seeking

And when I look there is a dream,
Both eyes behold the present scene.

But then I hear, and nothing's there
For sound intrudes upon the air.

And tasting sweet distil libations
Clothing sense with limitations.

Yet still, still calling unto me
Says search, unveil this mystery.

For all around and ever near
Is work and word for us to hear.

—o()o—

One of the apparent difficulties which humanity faces is
that which might be called the 'want' process. The Creation
is there (here) to meet the needs of everyone. Once there is
the acquirement of something over and above your needs,

that is equivalent to theft.

Meanwhile, for those of us who feel the need for an awareness beyond our present unconscious (dreaming) state, let us try this simple experiment. Find a quiet place; ask for no disturbance if necessary; rest within yourself. Allow your thoughts to pass by your mind. If outside noises should intervene, watch how 'something' goes to them or imagine their form, but try to allow them to be. They are just noises, and to shoo them away is just a distraction of negative energy. You can do a similar exercise in the countryside or at sea. After a while, take a slow, deep breath, hold it for a few seconds and then breathe out.

We all need to rest. Constant agitation is just wasted activity (energy). It is important to understand that everything which is created arises in the all embracing stillness. Everything that exists is born in one form or another, whether it is born of nature or the hands of man. Everything arises from within the silence and falls back into the silence.

The male partner injects his sperm into the female and, within her, the creative existence arises and is then ejected into the perceived space. That which is to be is ejected into this stillness, this silent capacity, and matures by using available resources of a manifest nature. So, in the grand manner of life, a Creative Principle injects a seed (idea) into this apparent void (mind) and a new form is born. So the birth process of our children replicates the birth of all things as ONE ongoing principle.

Here, there, begins the point of remembering this part of one's journey arising from the birth (Christ and Mary) back to the source. In this period, one is the servant of the Creative Principle and is being asked to help in the forward motion of creation. No servant becomes the work; he does the work. He waits to see what is needed or is called to do what is needed and then gets on with this work, but does not become the work itself.

Now think to yourself how many animals can construct their own residences. We know that beavers can construct a dam of sorts and hermit crabs occupy empty shells. Some hibernate in makeshift tunnels, and birds build nests. Ants do have a house of sorts.

Here then is a human weakness. But the body, as it were, is home for this True Being, an entity of higher spiritual value. It has a value by which it is connected to the Creative Will. It can motivate bodily action and watch that action taking place. And, in a world of duality, it can offer negative or positive forces of power. It can guide the body to construct and create in similar but very small ways to that of creation. Given positive energy forces, one edges closer to the central principle often referred to as God, Allah, Jehovah, Brama or the Creator, from where it obtains its sustaining force. A positive alignment with the centre will bring a more fruitful and enjoyable existence, whilst negative thoughts leading to retarding circumstances can take one into unhappy and often disastrous areas of life's environment.

If we can accept that mankind has been given such fundamental qualities of progressive action then it is reasonable to suppose that any action which is in opposition to the Creative Principle will receive a redirected force or punishment for so doing.

In conclusion, therefore, we are led to conclude that mankind is given this mystical power for a simple reason: to help progress creation forward. Yet, after centuries of gradual development, there are still these entities which preach for contrary action causing hardship, cruelty and destruction.

In the Christian tradition, Jesus, the Son of God died up on the cross and thus, by shedding His life, the redemption of our sins is promised. However, 'I find no sin in this,' said Pontius Pilate, and yet the public issue prevailed. It is also for consideration that He was considered to be a nuisance to the authorities. Whatever the case, He carried his cross to Golgotha and died. We all carry the burden of the cross, and can only find forgiveness if we bear it with humility.

—o0o—

When something terrible happens, many people say to each other: 'If there is a God, why does He let this happen?' This is a perfectly relevant question except, of course, we do not know the answer.

There are some possibilities which we could consider:

Maybe an individual brought it on themselves and needed to be taught a lesson

Maybe people in society had taken shortcuts in working practices

Possibly one authority had not heeded a warning

Maybe an individual was being foolhardy and 'flying in the face' of nature

These are all cases where the cause can be ascertained, but there is so much we do not know that it is foolishness to blame God for something which we have no knowledge about at all.

Many may die as a result of a misdemeanour or accident so that many others may live if the lesson is accepted. Have not, for example, developments in car design through experience resulted in safer vehicles? Ships were wrecked until we thought of lighthouses. Land lay dormant until a dam was built to assist in providing water for irrigation. If one studies books on history, it is possible to see how creation gradually opens up like a freshly blooming flower.

What is sad is that continuing lessons are still not learned.

There is a reason for every single happening.

–o0o–

Let us use our imagination for a while
Sit quietly, stay where you are
And imagine everyone doing the same
There was no change in your perception
Wherever you travelled
Where you are today, would you enjoy that?
Maybe you would be bored
Surely the answer is to accept diversity
And learn to share the enjoyment of differences
No criticism; no fighting
Just accept that which is.

–o0o–

If it was not so shocking, the following story would almost be unbelievable:

An émigré from a Middle Eastern country, given haven and sanctuary in a Western European state, is found to be denouncing those in the West for killing his fellow religious followers when the latter are murdering and maiming their own kind by the score or more each month. Without claiming that one side has right on its side, it is hard to comprehend the blatant and damaging hypocrisy being proffered to young citizens. Surely, as the Christian Bible suggests, anyone should consider the mote in their own eye before casting aspersions about others. It is bigots of this kind who cause so much ill-feeling between different echelons of society.

–o0o–

One of the interesting facts of life is the wave-like fortunes of existence. This is particularly noticeable in the case of fashion in whatever form. This wave-like rhythm applies to all conditions of substance and, in what might be termed a midway condition, concerns empires and civilisations. It applies in business. Surely we all know it takes time and toil to build a solid, strong business culture but it can decline at a far quicker rater than it took to build up. Trust is another example – built over time, it can be destroyed in one ill-conceived action.

—ₒ◯ₒ—

It is no good teaching others if you have not taught yourself. First, one has to know about oneself to understand others. With knowledge of self, compassion for others begins to grow and their needs become apparent.

—ₒ◯ₒ—

These are traditional English sayings:

1) Do not lose your temper. Control it. It is valueless
2) It matters not whether you win or lose, but how you play the game
3) Patience is a virtue. Learn from it, and hold to it if you can
4) Be positive; then look ahead
5) A wandering mind indicates a lost soul
6) Mark your aim. Stick to it on all occasions; otherwise you are aimless
7) Be respectful of another's need
8) Truth is indivisible. Hold fast to the truth
9) Trust once lost is never regained
10) Do not lie
11) Do not act your part in life. Watch it
12) Guidance is preferable to criticism which is negative
13) Moderation is a good motto (in all things)
14) Argument wastes energy. Deliberate
15) Choose your company with care and honour it
16) Take your shares and share the rest

17) Always start from where you are now
18) Faith, hope and love are great comforters in Truth
19) Your body is a gift. Treat it with respect
20) Care for all creatures
21) Treat thy neighbour as thyself
22) Should you fall, get up
23) Wallowing in mud makes you dirty
24) Love is a dual carriageway in one direction
25) Judge yourself before you judge others
26) You plough your own furrow. Don't blame others
27) Find your forte and develop it
28) In the heat of the moment, create a cool breeze
29) Be true to yourself

–o()o–

Guidance

When I first moved to the town I live in now, I rented for a year; then I wanted to buy a house. I knew what I wanted as far as rooms go, plus a carport and near the rural area but not in it. For a few weeks, I went to all the open houses in town to show the universe that I was serious about buying. Oh, did I mention that I wasn't working as I had been rear-ended by a semi a few months upon arrival here? That didn't stop me. I had been working with my guides and the universe for years, so I had every faith that I could do it. I had enough money for a down payment from the sale of my previous house, so I could move here with my son.

I decided to make it concrete, so off I went downtown and went into a real estate office. I told the woman what I wanted and how much I wanted to pay. She said there wasn't anything in town that remotely resembled what I wanted at the price I wanted to pay, and she could get me a place for that in the next town over. I didn't want to live in that other town; I wanted to live here, I said. She said she couldn't help me.

I went out of her office, contemplated things for a few minutes, then walked across the street to another real estate office. I looked at the pictures of listings in the windows, and one caught my eye. I used my cellphone to call the realtor to ask about it (I hate salesmen so I didn't want to go inside) and he said the one I was looking at was one to tear down and rebuild. Did I want to come inside, he asked, to take a look at others? I was about to say no when a finger pushed into the middle of my upper back and began to push me towards the entrance door. I looked back and there was no one there, but I was being pushed into the office. I met the realtor expecting the same response as across the street, but he said to me, "How about if I can get you the house you want, and it will cost you less?" I couldn't believe my ears! I immediately said yes.

Within three weeks, he found me a three-bedroom house with a carport and a downstairs to put in a suite, all of which I'd had on my list, for less than what I first thought I would pay! Thank you to the guides that pushed me through his office door that day as he made my dreams come true!

Anon

The Whole Truth

The reader may think we are cynical when we say that those who believe as follows: *I swear to tell the truth, the whole truth and nothing but the truth*, etc just really have little or no idea of what they are saying. The number of people on this earth who know the whole Truth is very few. You can add to this: *As I believe it to be so*, and this would be more acceptable.

To understand this thought a little better, consider this: If there is a motor accident, the police appeal for witnesses. If there is a resulting trial, the witnesses appear in court. Why more than one? If that one swore on oath as requested, knowing the whole truth, there should be no need for any further witnesses. In fact, the whole truth would be evident without calling anyone at all.

–o()o–

Remembering

When I requested a comment on my latest manuscript, the critic replied that it would seem to be becoming rather repetitive of comments made in previous editions. This brought to mind the days at school when 2 x 2 = 4 would have to be repeated many times until it was properly remembered.

How often has it been said: Now remember what you did and don't do it or you will hurt yourself again.

It is a fact of life that if we do not remember what is needed to be remembered then you will receive constant reminders until the matter is resolved.

Remembering the lessons in life is part of the necessary way of improving our manner of living; of getting to know a little, or even quite a lot, about our important inner self.

It is so important to realise that there is a manifest world in which we, in our form as humans, spend our daily lives. Then there is a formless spiritual world of self-realisation which is in need of development and has to be practised and remembered, thus leading to pure Being.

—o○o—

Every human form in this world is the same, be it male or female. It is the human being that engages in different characteristics. As the great English playwright William Shakespeare wrote: To be or not to be, that is the question.

—o○o—

Can you not remember, we were told, we have said this once before? Maybe so, but did you remember? You see, one of the human problems is that everyone is so caught up in the 'affairs of man' that they forget the most important part of life which is to try and give attention to that which is not manifest. As has been written before, be guided by a good teacher who will show you the way. Further to this, we have noted previously that thought and mind (of use in the manifest world) create a form of barrier to further spiritual development. Nevertheless, they do play a very important role in everyday life.

One needs to watch and follow how the mind reacts to certain events. It is so very important to participate in and enjoy life in a positive way. Watch out for negative thinking. So many of us rest in an energy field of negative thinking that we never get anywhere at all. One has to find, through experience, a way of **I can do** and not **that cannot be done**. Or maybe it is better this way than the one suggested. There has to be a balanced judgement in these matters.

Think for a moment – would all the major inventions over the centuries have been made if the inventors were burdened with negative thinking? Positive thinking directed properly leads to a much happier and fulfilling life.

Boundaries

Human beings need boundaries. Without boundaries, we would bo in chaos. This applies to relationships as it does to players on a cricket field. It not only applies to people but also to countries, and such boundaries should be agreed by all parties concerned. This is well worth remembering and should certainly be taught to young people. In other words, there are times when one has to show self-restraint.

Linda Smith

Many of us will have experienced the force of gravity when standing on the edge of a high cliff or from the edge of a high building. Normally we are not aware of this force and its power; likewise, the force of love and happiness which beckons continuously but remains somewhat hidden. One can become aware of it by giving it our attention in many ways.

—o()o—

There is no end to a new beginning.

—o()o—

There is a trap door and an open door. Make the right steps forward.

—o()o—

If you love one another, what more do you need?

—o()o—

Keep an open mind but guard the entrance

–o()o–

It may well be noted that everybody is the same – worldwide (human – male/female). Furthermore, of course, given wider consideration, there is duality in the shape of FORM, for example: black and white; light and dark; hard and soft; thick and thin; and so on.

Now, let us divert our attention for a while. Purchase a bag of boiled sweets and examine the content. Every sweet is the same but the flavouring is different – lime, raspberry, blackcurrant, etc. Why is this? It is because each sweet has been subjected to a different flavouring or, as is the case with the human FORM, different climatic conditions, family environment, and so many other surrounding conditions.

This variety should become a matter of interest and not contention, realising everybody is the same at the beginning. But then this duality situation arises again in that which is form – of this world and that which is spiritual or formless. The alternative is to match the two together in the natural state of one complete whole. This is the human personality, understanding the need for self-realisation, and the sharing and enjoyment of appearances, and not being antagonistic towards them. There is the everlasting stillness in which all this occurs. Seek it. Find it.

–o()o–

However clever the professor may be, he does not know as much as the prophet.

–o()o–

He who has the sweetest tooth may not have the finest tongue.

—o()o—

Be thankful for your present blessings
Do not count the future to come

—o()o—

There is a law for the rich and another
for the poor in spirit.

—o()o—

The key to the treasure chest lies in the heart.

—o()o—

Everyone needs a goal but some do not kick the ball.

—o()o—

Every morning, between the hours of eight to half past eight, Dod, a large black and white male cat, and his two daughters align themselves on the terrace furniture for breakfast; wild cats awaiting sustenance for their bodies. After eating, they vanish until the middle of the afternoon when they return again for the final meal of the day.

There are those who offer prayers of thanks on a similar basis for the gift of life, but how many of us do not even bother to say thank you once in a week?

Two good meals and a comfortable place to lie down are gifts of a worldly price; beyond this is the gift of companionship with the Creator.

—o()o—

Has it ever occurred to you that in the manifest world every body feeds another body? Without going into minute detail, let us follow this concept in its broadest sense:

The earth is granted sunlight and rain
Grasses, herbs and trees feed on the earth
Insects, animals and humans feed on the growth of form
The seas follow a similar pattern

Humans go a stage further for they feed off almost everything else. Therefore, the big question is: Who feeds with us?

—o()o—

The above is not really new: both scientific and biological discoveries are uncovering more and more of the diversity of human nature and the living world. In fact, it would be better for all of us to pay more attention to the eco-system than the ego-system.

—o()o—

It is sad to see so many individuals apparently travelling in a straight line but just going round in circles. It is quite a dilemma.

—o()o—

The way to transform our habitual reactions is to bring a positive attitude to every situation and feel the positive energy deeply.

—o()o—

There is, in truth, no duality. This is how the manifestation of form appears to be but, in the absence of form, there is only one, and this is expressed in the words: There is ONE.

—o()o—

In the theatre, each actor is given their role to play. So it is for each one of us in life. The scenery is set before us, almost static in the theatre but constantly in a state of movement in life. Find the peace in which the movement takes place.

—o()o—

Road signs – read carefully for future guidance

The sign indicates	Significance
Dangerous bend	Do be careful
Speed limit...	Go too fast and overlook opportunities
Double white lines	Avoid argument
Level crossing	Be watchful of your actions
Roundabout ahead	There are many ways
No parking	Avoid entrapment in false premises
One way	There is only one way
Road narrows	Path may be difficult to traverse
Dual carriageway	One way ahead
Stop	Look and listen
Crossroads	It is your choice

—o()o—

There has to be a shared understanding

Most of us will know that 'two wrongs' do not make 'a right' – then again, 'two rights' do not make 'a wrong'. What, of course, is more difficult to understand is the problem with '*I am right and he is wrong*'.

It is obvious that there can only be one complete Truth and that a true teaching is one way for those who seek to find it. So it may be argued that there can be more than one True Teaching given to humanity to find the Whole Truth-Creator. If we go back to schooldays, we may find, say, a language was taught one way by one teacher and in a different way by another. Yet the aim for the pupil is the same. Although there may be a similarity, there is a difference in how a teacher propounds his subject to listeners. As there are practical examples, should we not consider the probability that similar principles apply to the teachings of the search for Truth? Perhaps tolerance and understanding of the way in which others work is more appropriate. Of course, there are false doctrines, but any person understanding the truth in their heart, not intolerance, should be aware of the conscious presence of Truth.

–o()o–

Only recently, I was sitting quietly on my own when a Latin verb came to mind. This can be a little difficult to comprehend because it was eighty years ago that I closed the book whose content did not exactly excite me. Soon afterwards, I was reading a book in which it was stated that happiness is a state of mind and not a condition of circumstances. To me, this was a very bold statement. Nevertheless, I leave this open to individual thinking. However, I will remember a lady friend of mine who was continually finding fault with every one of her business colleagues, so much so that I found fault with her and closed down the relationship. Living in a retirement home, there was a lady here as well whose attitude about others was also negative. One could almost feel the curtain of dark mist which enveloped her whole person. All this negativity means the ordinary individual does not like to associate with the person concerned.

–o()o–

It is often said of modern-day living: 'These are testing times.'

What about yourself? Do you have testing times?

Here are some highly relevant quotations from people who have been noted for their great wisdom, and their knowledge and consciousness stands firm for all.

As a man thinketh in his heart, so is he.
King Solomon, 10BC

I pray Thee, O God, that I may be beautiful within.
Socrates, 469-399BC

Keep a good tongue in your head.
William Shakespeare, 1564-1616

All that we are is the result of what we have thought.
Buddha c560-480BC

Our life is simply what our thoughts make of it.
Marcus Aurelius 121-180

You will see from these quotations that many are, as they say, 'as old as the hills'. Maybe, but truth never changes. It is always truth. So can we be practical and find that *turning point* to change ourselves along the Path of Truth? Let us, for a moment, consider how we may think:

Do we talk others down to uplift ourselves?

Do we think we are right and others always wrong? Even if they are, be gentle.

Do we listen or continually interrupt?

We do not have to agree but we need not be insulting.

Is our thinking always negative or can it become positive?

One may learn from mistakes. Better to give guidance than ridicule.

Do you think you know all the answers? Ah!!

These are just questions you might ask yourself, but no doubt there are many others. Few if any of us are perfect, but a little 'polish and clean up' might help to brighten the lives of those with whom you associate. To turn and look in another direction may also grant you more joy and happiness.

Life repeats itself in one form or another until the lesson is accepted and acted upon. Let us think of simple instances:

Put too much water into the cementing process and the result is weakness

Tell a lie, and lose a trust

Be jealous and lose a friend

Plant your seeds at the wrong time and diminish or even lose your crop

Do you really know the answer, or think you do?

–o()o–

Maybe, later in life, you will be able to understand that events you did not like or appreciate were, in fact, a guiding force to help you find the True Path to Self-Realisation.

Perhaps, therefore, if you are a young individual, you may remember this and work in true faith from the negative event.

—o〇o—

When there is so much beauty in the world, why is there so much unhappiness? Is it because of man's greed, his selfishness, fear and delusion?

—o〇o—

If you are interested in the origin of the species then why not consider what is right with the species and where it went wrong. After all, we have been given a great gift. Did we want more?

—o〇o—

One can point to many instances in people's lives when, for instance, a *turning point* arises: a change of job or a marriage are just two instances when one's life has to change. Can we accept that the really crucial case is where one discovers the critical turning point and one discovers the differences between the fragile covering of form and the fundamental nature of the formless?

—o〇o—

One is given a life on this planet to enhance the development of the creative and spiritual force. It is not to enhance selfish desires and egoistic principles.

—o〇o—

The first lesson in life is to live in the present moment – NOW. Secondly, you are here to assist with the Creator's Will, whatever that might be. In doing so, you have to sublimate your ego and always try and adopt a true and positive life projection. In so doing, you will not only wittingly or even unwittingly help others but you will also find your own life actions will be more positive and good for your own inward joy and happiness.

Remember you must trust your Creator and guidance is for the long-term future; not necessarily what you want at this present moment.

—o()o—

Argument

How many of us truly consider the value of expressive energy? However, we can possibly appreciate the explosive use of energy in having an argument with another person. Have you ever thought how wasteful this can be and how better time would be spent on doing something useful.

At the time of writing these few words, there is a civil war being fought in a Middle Eastern country: two 'states' with opposing views. After two years, nearly 100,000 have been killed, thousands wounded, and millions have fled the country. Beautiful towns and ancient monuments are in ruins. All because parties or collectives have different views. One can well see the terrible work of energy which could have served the opposite purpose of bringing better living conditions and happier lives to those in torment.

Now, look at nature – nature in front of us. There too are what appear to be opposites: thick and thin; wet and dry; hot and cold. In all these is a middle way; in all these, there is a third force of energy pulsating with them. Isn't it true that human beings, whoever they may be and whatever status they may hold, learn to understand that there is a balance in everything, and that that balance means compromise and sharing of the natural order, whether as husband and wife, brother and sister, or nation and its neighbour. There always has to be a balance of understanding. We still have a lot to learn and practise.

—o〇o—

Can you change your thinking pattern? Or are you set in your existing pattern?

—o〇o—

He who preaches like a zealot may be beside himself. He who preaches in moderate temperament may be beside us all.

—o〇o—

It matters not what you think. It is who you are that counts.

—o〇o—

There is nothing to stop you from being beautiful within except your own self.

—o〇o—

Space is so joyful, so peaceful and quiet
That which is within it moves
But the magnitude remains still

—o〇o—

Those who conquer perish
Those who love persist

—o〇o—

Let us agree, as has been said, 'It's a wonderful world.' Now the point to remember is that we have been given a part to play in it, but we do not own it. Any part of our gift, and that includes ourselves, can be taken away at any time. One has to find out by whom or by what. It is necessary to acknowledge this factor. Otherwise, one's life cycle will be unworthy of the opportunity.

We can easily accept that people wear different clothes from one another. They live under different circumstances, and the clothes may change with circumstances. It is similar with belief. But, finally, there is only one Truth.

There is a historical expression '*All roads lead to Rome*'. At that time, Rome was the capital of the old Roman Empire. You can say that all true religions lead to Home.

Humans used to be taught the principle that matter is life. They are supposed to recognise the Truth and help to cultivate it. They are not supposed to become self-indulgent, intolerant and egocentric. So it may be said that the principle of life commences from being a human to a human being: A Being that just IS in the present moment. As humans, we have many faults. As human beings, we are learning to develop a higher standard of understanding, awareness and what actually IS.

The richness of life is not about money or possessions. If you have all you need, you are rich indeed but the real point of the situation is knowing what you need – acceptance of what is; less attachment to materialistic matters and consciousness of what the body is; forgetting the insubstantial, ephemeral world of form for the ever present and formless eternal spiritual dimension in which everything rests.

Now you may say we have read all this before, but note, there is a forgetting, and constant reminding is necessary even when the rhythm of life has completely changed.

—o0o—

In ageing years, how comforting it is to be remembered by relatives and friends.

There is a deeper meaning to life than just living.

One may know how but do we know about when?

One needs to look beyond the object to observe the emanation.

Did you know that doctrine can become dogma?

Nothing in this manifest world matches the beauty and harmony of the spiritual.

What mankind has lost, we can but imagine.

You say 'thank you' for your life. By helping others; by loving others.

It is not important what you know, but who you know that counts. For, if you keep good company, you will learn to know what you know.

If one did not grow older and possibly wiser, one would be dead.

How often is it easier to be told what to do than doing it.

Do I have to make a noise to be acknowledged?

It is not a good state of affairs when a man thinks he knows best.

Come what may, may yet come.

Here today and gone tomorrow.
Here today and gone forever.
Here and now, always.

There is one way – and One way only.

It is a long journey to here until you have travelled.

Faith will find what brains cannot reveal.

There is no end to the beginning.

Keep every action simple.

The only one who loses is the one who possesses.
A sceptic was asked: 'Are you saying that, because you cannot see it, it does not exist?'

She was too young to be my daughter
I was too old to be her father
How the years pass on
Maybe the eye is never dim

Everything manifested is ephemeral including pleasure which is only a guide to happiness which rests in the silence of the soul.

And when the rains came, the odour of the earth was beautiful. So refreshing, so cooling after the long, hot summer days.

The spirit of the great may appear to be stronger than that of the weak. This is not right, so far as the spirit is concerned, it is the same, and it is just taking longer to mature.

No matter what job has to be performed, one needs the correct tools, properly cared for, and one must work properly.

You gallop away from the oasis only to find the desert.

It is not what one learns that is important. It is experience which matters and that needs work of the Spirit.

Simplicity is the essence. Simplicity is substantial.

I suddenly understood that I had a long way to travel but nowhere to go.

Have you noticed that every living thing contains the seed of its own renewal?

Observe the motion picture of life. Do not LIVE in it.

One has to learn that which no one can teach you.

We love the bees; we love the birds; we love the blossom
But it is the essence, perfume or fragrance which lives on.

It is not easy to see how the egos of a few cause the suffering
of many others.

It is not the body that makes one beautiful. View its
function rather than its form.

Failure is when one gives up totally. Love dispels fear.

Do not deceive yourself into believing who you are.

Remember that any enterprise is only as good as the people
who work in it.

The pain of possession is an aching heart.

Success is a straightforward path of many small steps.

Are you so fond of yourself that you cannot trust your body
in the hands of the Merciful?

You decide what is to come in this present moment.

—o()o—

How many of us realise that this world is a wonderful gift
given to us to share with the Giver or Creator? So why is
it over the passage of time that we expend so much energy
in destructive activities and wasteful expenditure when all
that effort could have been spent on enhancing the beauty
and joy towards happiness for everyone? The problem,
it would seem, lies in those whose greed and selfishness
leads to the disappointment of others. It matters not how
this disastrous trait is displayed; it always leads to tragedy,
whether it is international, local or individual. We forget
that love in the creation is for sharing that gift and not for

squandering it.

—o()o—

That which is born in the heart surpasses the mind.

—o()o—

He who steals from his brother
Demeans himself far more than he takes.

—o()o—

Peace of mind is a piece of paradise.

—o()o—

This really is a beautiful world. So give this question a little thought: Why are we, as human beings, being 'brought in' to live in it? There has to be something or someone who creates it and keeps it going, so it is not really difficult to understand that there is a Creator, and a great number of human beings, whatever their background, worship, in one form or another, a Higher Being.

It might, therefore, be a good question to ask ourselves: What are we here for? What is our purpose? Given our natural abilities, it is not difficult to consider that our true purpose as humans is to help with the continuation of the beautiful planet plus as human beings to glory in the spiritual sanctity of the Creator and His purpose.

Why not give this idea some thought and consider what you can do in a positive way to help in this creation and avoid the destructive nature of so much negative influence being applied through selfishness, greed and self-aggrandisement.

A positive contribution from any individual could make a real difference however minute it might appear to be.

Recall that every object starts as a seed from somewhere.

—o()o—

True friendship is a great teacher for learning
how to share.

—o()o—

You are human, are you not? One small atom of the crowd which is called humanity. But the real question is 'Are you a human being?' Are you being helpful to others, compassionate, kind and thoughtful; existing in true conscious spirit.

True Being is a spiritual gift given to everyone, and everyone receives this gift. But ask yourselves: 'Do we truly use and share it?'

To become a human being is your life's work – a messenger from the Creator to undertake His Will.

—o()o—

Take it as you like it, says one. But this may not
be what you need.

—o()o—

My friend did not die. It was his body that
ceased to function.

—o()o—

That which is present is forever.

—o()o—

Happiness only ever is in the present moment, so it is up to you to make it so.

—o()o—

Live NOW and live forever. Living in the future is a no-win situation.

—o()o—

Society wants power. Individuals want power. This only leads to disruption. For there is only one source of creative power, and that is spiritual power above all. Lack of understanding leads to the problem which civilisation has faced and still does. One can enjoy power without greed and selfishness.

—o()o—

Surely there are two very interesting questions which each of us needs to answer. They are:

Who are you?
Why are you here?

Let us deal with the last one first. Are we, as individuals, here

to help in the development of the Creation?
for our own improvement?
to satisfy ourselves?

If you adopt the last position, you are not really helping anyone. Perhaps you might consider that the first true option might work together and this poses the question of '*Who are you*?' again.

—o()o—

It makes you think about a thing or two. Have you ever really considered what happens when one 'thing' meets another 'thing' in the warmth and cover of a mother's womb? Have you ever thought that these two 'things' actually have the necessary skills and facilities to bring about the beginning of a human body? A body with all the complicated moving and active parts; the ability to see, hear, taste, breathe. Each result is a miracle. Surely this and all the other miracles in creation deserve some respect.

—o()o—

There is no end to the beginning without
another beginning.

—o()o—

A wise saying like the falling leaves of autumn provides
new sustenance to the recipient.

—o()o—

Truth has a presence beyond fact.

—o()o—

Think of the beauty of a single flower. Then consider how
intelligence has fashioned so many different varieties. No
one can make such wonder on their own.

—o()o—

How long will it take for us to accept WHO we are, and
not believe in who we think we are?

—o()o—

There is a love which passeth all understanding. For it even
loves the poorest, the weakest, and the most vulnerable.
Assuredly, this is our guide.

—o()o—

If one is receptive to the feeling that the Being provides
better than 'ME' then the level of redemption changes.
One recognises the wholeness of ONE; not just one self
and everything else.

—o()o—

The Turning Point is towards the still point.

—o()o—

Activities in life should lead towards Truth,
not to selfish ends.

—o()o—

There is a world problem, and we can all help to solve
it. This amounts to the non-recognition of the Spirit. It
is covered over by endless thinking, and the false use of
mind. Become ego-less.

—o()o—

Signal your intention
Practise what you truly believe.

—o()o—

Every turning point, in the right direction,
leads to a new life.

—o()o—

'That's the way it is' is a really important statement.
Acceptance.
Move on from there in a positive direction.

—o()o—

Do we act to our own desires and ego, or through the
strength which lies behind this covering?

—o()o—

If you really see your little self, you can begin to see your
True self.

—o()o—

Truthfully speaking, life is really not difficult to understand. It is we who complicated it. Our, what you might refer to as, ego personalities are always trying to be better than someone else. It is always 'me' against the others. (Look at zealots or dictators.) Such thinking disturbs the equilibrium and breeds disharmony. So it is that our thinking is responsible for the disturbed mind. We need to rest our feelings in the very nature of life. Help me to fulfil the creative purpose; not: it is 'I' when I am above all others in deciding what action is necessary.

—o0o—

I was told that a learned professor once said: 'And when the dinosaurs died out 100,000,000 years ago, a new era started.' How does that relate to your age and what you are supposed to know? It puts life into perspective, doesn't it? Even the president of the largest nation or the managing director of the world's largest corporation is insignificant in this comparative relationship; in relation to the creative process, apparently very little. But then, think again – just one mosquito can kill a human; a small leak in a vessel's hull can sink a big ship; and a volcanic eruption can cost thousands of lives.

Surely the answer is: Is your contribution to the progress of evolution a positive and constructive attribute to the developing organism? Love thy neighbour as thyself.

—o0o—

Is it not a fact that memories of past events can be evocative of a fundamental truth even though brought to mind many years after they occur?

On this occasion, I recall an incident in 1944 when I was an officer in the Indian Army under the temporary command of an American general; the only British officer, in fact, at the jungle airfield which we had just recaptured from the enemy. Several miles away, across the wide river and in the Burmese jungle, was a brigade of our troops, the Chindits, and it was important that these troops assisted in speeding up the advance of our troops against the retreating enemy.

I was given a message to take to the jungle warriors. A plane and pilot was provided, and I was flown to the jungle airstrip on the border with China. On arrival, I was introduced to two local natives from N Burma who were to take me to the location where the British commander was awaiting orders. This they did.

We had no means of verbal communication. We could possibly have been ambushed at any time, but these two little men, totally uneducated, took me to the right destination so that I could deliver the general's message.

Truthfully, it showed how we really can help each other if we know how to and want to do so. I was not brave, but I placed my life in the trusted hands of these two men whose bodies were bare except for a loincloth, and whose weapons were wooden stakes.

Let us not forget the importance of other folks, even though they might not sit on the pinnacles of power.

—o0o—

One of the amazing aspects of life on this planet is that humanity has not yet learned to accept that not everyone has the same approach to a particular subject – in this case, religion.

There is an obvious, clear and simple statement to all. In visiting Central Africa, people wear a different style of dress to others. In London, England, policemen wear a different uniform to that of Canadian or US police.

We can apply this idea all over the world. Nevertheless,

each individual has a body similar to that of another individual except that there are 'covers' which are different because, for example, of local conditions. Bodily functions of a man or a woman are similar, just covered over by different clotheswear.

The great majority of the world population hold to the idea of a strong, superior natural force. As with clothes, the experience of this force depends on the conditions which surround the individual person, and how he/she receives these conditions. This force is hidden behind a curtain of continuous thought and mental agitation. Keep things simple. Whatever our interpretation of a particular stage of development, everything is the same (ONE) but different. Let us take the European Continent as an example: As at 2013 AD, there are twenty-three different nationalities. They are trying to formulate policies suitable for all.

—o()o—

Everything grows in the space the Creator provides.

—o()o—

You may be worldly wise and that is where you stay.

—o()o—

Every human being is equal except where they disqualify themselves from being so, but so few qualify to be so.

—o()o—

Green Shoots – Talent

My name is Sabrine. I was born in the UK and I am almost eighteen. I live in Spain now. I left school when I was fifteen, one year before I was able to get the Spanish leavers' certificate. Even though I have always disliked going to a Spanish school because of the difficulty of learning the language, since the age of seven I've had a passion for singing.

I've recently composed my own personal songs by guitar and lyrics, and I'm in the process of composing for the rest of the instruments. I hope to publish my songs soon (have my CD).

When I write the songs, I spend hours, sometimes days. It's like something or someone else gives me the lyrics inside my head to make a song not only for me but more importantly to inspire others who may or may not have the same dream as me to sing. But the messages I give out are mainly for everyone to believe in themselves with whatever dreams they have.

I know within myself that I will be who I want to be, and it has taken me a long while to believe in myself, not to mention all the years wasted, including my talent. Low self-confidence stopped me from doing what I love but now, since I've discovered my talent in writing music, nothing can stop me. It took me all this time to realise I was good at writing my songs, but when I write I give all I feel inside onto that sheet of paper.

If only everyone could discover they are good at something, which everybody really is, they would make so much out of themselves, because talent is a gift, and the worst thing is truly wasted talent. The message I want to give out is that everybody has a purpose in life. Some of us have had bad experiences in our lives and those have knocked our confidence and self-worth, but if you have a dream and desire, know that this is probably your purpose in life: to be the person you dream of being – author, singer, dancer, actor, gardener, teacher, etc. You are doing it because it's your passion, but you are also changing lives and giving your all to it.

And if you haven't yet discovered your talent, it's there. Just look deep within yourself, possibly with the help of meditation. If you are spiritual like me, you will, or you shouldn't have a problem seeking the answer to your question of what your talent is. There is a lot more to life than we are aware of. From my spiritual experiences and meditation, I have had a lot of help writing music and believing in myself.

Don't let past experiences stop you from being who you are meant to be. Nothing is your fault. We all deserve to be happy and sometimes need to push ourselves whether we like it or not.

Sabrine

If all you do is to consider yourself as a body moving around in a world of matter then, one would ask, what is your life cycle? Surely you as a person with sense must be respectful of more than that. And truly who really are you?

—o0o—

Your Life

Be still for a moment. Sit upright and do not lounge. Give consideration to that which is to follow. At this stage, do not provoke an argument.

Stage 1

We live in a Creation. This is a form of universal consciousness which obviously has a Creator, everything which is being created, and the active force which is creating.

Stage 2

This implies a 3 in 1 principle: acceptance of a superior being (Creator); humanity as being an active principle; and the energy which drives the development.

Stage 3

The Creator provides all the necessary fundamentals and requires us to conform to his wishes.

Stage 4

The journey on the earth is granted so that we may behold its majesty and, in simple ways, we are shown the way.

Stage 5

The first lesson we need to learn is that we all live in the present moment. There is no other moment. Time has been made for human convenience. What IS just IS. That which has gone is the past and, whilst one may consider it often or what is to come, it always IS. If needs be, this ISness can be changed by work in the present moment.

Stage 6

So what you do now dictates what one becomes, and one can only start from where one is – the present.

Stage 7

So we arrive at this: it is not what you want; it is what is needed both for yourself and the universal progress.

Stage 8

This is the *Turning Point* when one becomes aware of WHAT IS, accepts that ISness, and realises the personal need for change of direction in one's own life in a positive manner.

—o0o—

Conclusion

In days long gone, the parents of a small boy placed a framed motto on the mantelpiece of his bedroom. The motto read something like this: 'When the one great scorer comes to write against your name, he writes not whether you won or lost but how you played the game.'

Perhaps it is time for each one of us to read these words for they have the deepest of meanings. In the materialistic attitudes of people in this world today, maybe as a reader of this book, we can ask ourselves if we are playing the game according to the right rules: love, hope and charity in their broadest meaning. Maybe this is your '*Turning Point*' even by using it in the simplest of ways.

—o()o—

This may be the conclusion of this book in the series, but it is by no means the conclusion of your journey. May you receive encouragement and further spiritual strength, and find a willingness to share with others the joy and happiness which you have been given.

Other Books By Bernard Fillayson

In The Shade Of The Carob Tree

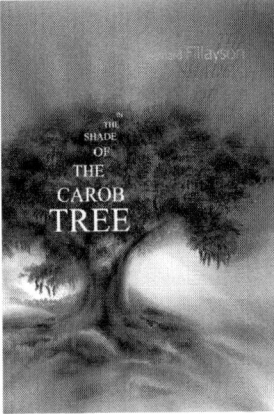

Why the Carob Tree you will ask?

Well, the tree gives a harvest of edible food pods. These pods have a high nutritional value and after processing the powder, it is used as a sweetener in many everyday products.

These attributes have been known for centuries, like the content of this book, but we need to be reminded of the value of such attributes which can bring us closer to joy, understanding and peace.

The nutritional value of learning from this reading can help the reader to enjoy a happier, more fulfilled life.

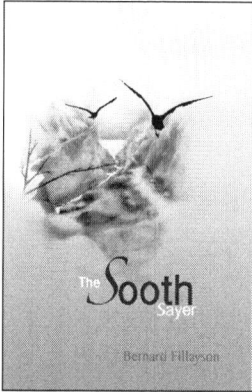

This book is about living our lives to the full. It could also be about changing the life we experience to one of greater natural fruitfulness.

The Tree of Life can bear two fruits: One is bitter and the other sweet. He who eats the bitter fruit seeks nothing but personal gain and ephemeral pleasures, whilst he who eats the sweeter fruit is granted a greater understanding of himself and others. Life becomes a happier experience and is in balance. It is the light of understanding and knowledge that is in the taste of the sweetened fruit for it brings greater happiness and contentment to the human heart and soul, leading to a more tranquil and harmonious life.

The Soothsayer offers every reader a taste of the sweetened fruit to take with them on their journey, to seek that love and beauty which resides within.

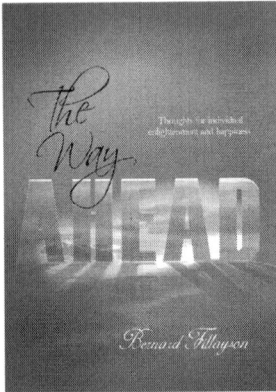

Whenever one goes on a journey, it is necessary to plan ahead. The Way Ahead provides outline planning for the journey of day-to day living. It indicates the way to seek and find that deeper meaning in life which leads to contentment and full understanding: a way out of human suffering and discontent.

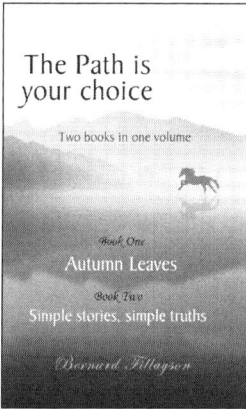

Autumn Leaves

This book offers the reader over one hundred short stories and more than four hundred aphorisms. All are connected with daily thoughts and living.

They are presented to the reader as an aid to search beyond the ego and touch the True Self which is within us all. They are signposts on the Path to Self-Fulfilment.

Simple stories, simple truths

Over one hundred simple stories and ideas taken from everyday life, together with guiding quotations from sources over a period of five millennia. These give a lead into much desired knowledge.

Translated into daily practice they provide guidance towards a happy and contented life for the wandering soul.

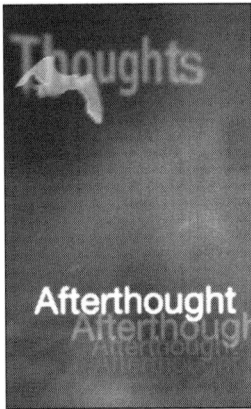

"No matter who you are or where you are, somewhere in the reading there is a message for you. It is of no consequence what one's religious or non-religious beliefs may be. Rather, it has a value for life; a value for contentment; for peace and reassurance. It is up to each intuitive reader to seek what they need."

This book contains many thought-provoking quotes from sources of great wisdom, from modern and ancient times.

www.bernardfillayson.com

5911729R00067

Printed in Great Britain
by Amazon.co.uk, Ltd.,
Marston Gate.